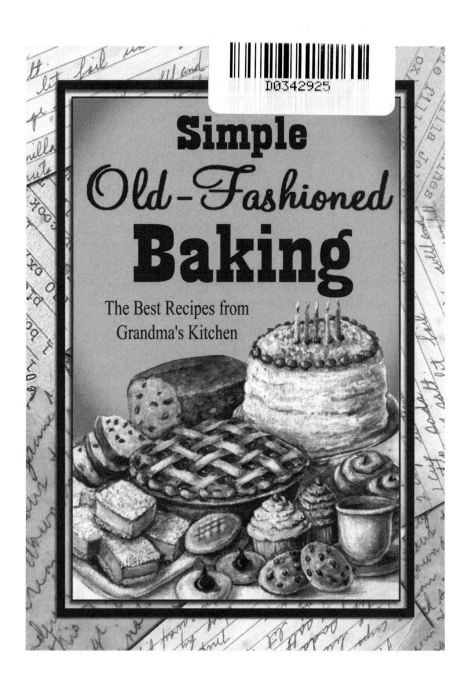

Simple
Old-Fashioned
Baking

The Best Recipes from
Grandma's Kitchen

Cookbook Resources, LLC
Highland Village, Texas

Simple Old-Fashioned Baking
The Best Recipes from Grandma's Kitchen

1ˢᵗ Printing–September 2008

International Standard Book No. 978-1-59769-032-4

Library of Congress No. 2008030236

Library of Congress Cataloging-in-Publication Data

Simple old-fashioned baking : the best recipes from Grandma's kitchen. -- 1st ed.
p. cm.
Includes index.
ISBN 978-1-59769-032-4
1. Baking. 2. Desserts. I. Cookbook Resources, LLC.
TX765.S525 2008
641.8'15--dc22

2008030236

Edited, Designed and Published in the
United States of America by
Cookbook Resources, LLC
541 Doubletree Drive
Highland Village, Texas 7507

Toll free 866-229-2665

www.cookbookresources.com

cookbook
resources® LLC
Bringing Family and Friends to the Table

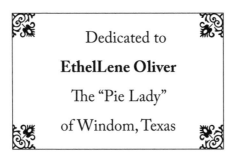

Dedicated to

EthelLene Oliver

The "Pie Lady"

of Windom, Texas

(Learn more about the "Pie Lady" on page 5.)

Introduction

The kitchens of our mothers, grandmothers and great-grandmothers were filled with the delicious aromas of freshly baked goods. From pies to bread to cakes, cookies and more, this book contains proven, time-honored recipes that fulfill our every craving for simple, old-fashioned baking.

These special treats are made from scratch and reflect our love not just of baking but of sharing yummy desserts, biscuits, brownies, candies and other goodies with our family and friends. There are short recipes and more elaborate ones – it's your choice of what you'd like to make – with love.

There are many ways we can show our love for family, and good cooking and baking are something they'll always remember and treasure.

Were you first to line in scrape the mixing bowl? Did you ever try to sneak around behind Mom's back to get at the cookie dough in the refrigerator? Did you tiptoe into the kitchen to get the last piece of pie? This book is for you!

Indulge yourself and enjoy!

Contents

The Pie Lady

EthelLene Oliver of Windom, Texas made pies for almost 30 years out of the kitchen of her turn-of-the-century farmhouse. In two of those years, she made 3,000 pies. If you figure conservatively at 2,500 pies per year for 25 years, it comes to 62,500 pies.

"I just picked up pie-making. Oh, I suppose I watched Momma when I was young; but really, I just started making pies," she says casually.

"I get up every morning around two o'clock to bake the pies and then take them over there [to son's Tommy's grocery store]. I make pies for other lunchrooms in the area and for folks who buy them for special occasions."

EthelLene first made pies for the public when her husband Kenneth, who was constable in Honey Grove, told his friends, Hoss and Georgia Luttrell, owners of Paula's Restaurant in Honey Grove, that EthelLene would be glad to help them out with a wedding reception by making eight lemon meringue pies. They were so good that Hoss figured he could sell the pies in his restaurant; so she starting making them and he started selling them.

Later when son Tommy bought the Windom grocery store in 1975, her pie-making increased dramatically. To help out the crews running the TPL railroad line from Savoy to Texarkana, Tommy opened a snack bar that quickly expanded to a lunch counter serving cheeseburgers and pie; PIE being the big draw. It wasn't long until EthelLene started making red beans and cornbread on Monday, stew and cornbread on Wednesday and chili on Friday...and, every day homemade PIES.

EthelLene made her pies from scratch. "I make my own crusts and I squeeze the lemons for lemon pie. Now that apricot, that's canned, because I don't have fresh or dried apricots. I have an aluminum pan I beat my egg whites in. The meringue won't stand up like that if I beat 'em in Tupperware, but I don't know if that's the reason they stand up like they do."

After baking 60 to 70 pies on any Thanksgiving eve or Christmas eve for other people, she always managed to get the turkey in the oven for her own family's special meals. "We have Thanksgiving dinner on Thanksgiving Day. We have Christmas dinner on Christmas Day. There hasn't been a Thanksgiving or Christmas dinner except at our house. The kids would all rather be here. It just wouldn't be the same if it weren't at Granny's. They all love to come home and we're all proud of that."

Windom is a town of 298 people and is located in Fannin County about half way between Bonham and Honey Grove and 80 miles northeast of Dallas. EthelLene has made pies for everyone in a three-county area and beyond. Every time there was a birth or death or special birthday party, she was at the door with her special pies that always made people feel better. The Pie Lady's fame has spread from Texas to California to New York City and lots of places in between.

The sister of one of EthelLene's daughters-in-law once visited with a stranger at a New York City airport who, after learning she was from Texas, told her she had to go Windom for a piece of homemade pie at Tommy Oliver's grocery store!

Newspaper and television reporters from all over Texas have come to Windom just to meet the Pie Lady, have a piece of pie and tell a story that's become a legend.

She and Kenneth were married for 55 years until he passed away. They had two sons and two daughters, seven grandchildren and, as of this writing, 15 great-grandchildren and 3 great-great-grandchildren. The Pie Lady is now 88 and has retired from making pies for others, but she still makes her grandchildren and great-grandchildren's favorite pies whenever they ask.

We dedicate this cookbook to EthelLene Oliver because she represents the best of America. Her strong family values, deep-rooted faith and love, kindness to others, personal happiness in serving others and always doing her utmost are among the treasures that make her so remarkable.

She put her best, her time and her heart into every pie she baked and we are thankful for her and others like her who make pies that somehow just make us feel better.

Pies
&
Tarts

Don't miss the special recipes by
the Pie Lady in this section!

Pies & Tarts Contents

Piecrust

A tender, flaky piecrust is the mark of an excellent baker. The perfect crust doesn't happen by accident. It takes practice and patience.

When making a crust, keep the following in mind. The butter (or fat) and liquid used in the crust should be ice cold. Room temperature butter or water will incorporate into the dough too completely, releasing gluten and producing a tougher crust. The ideal crust will have visible flecks of butter in it. These little leaves of butter are important for creating a flaky crust, once the dough has been put in the oven.

Handling the dough is just as important as the temperature of the ingredients. The dough should be mixed quickly, using as little liquid as possible, in order to create a dough that will just stick together.

Cutting the butter in with a knife or pulsing it in a food processor helps to "cut" the ingredients in, rather than "mixing" them. If using a food processor, do not over mix. Pulse judiciously, adding a tiny amount of liquid at a time. As soon as the dough forms a ball, it can be removed to the refrigerator to rest.

A perfectly uniform crust is not desirable, but there should not be giant lumps of unmixed flour, either. The goal is a happy medium, with little bits of butter here and there, and a dough that stays together.

The dough must rest for at least an hour before being rolled out. This allows the butter to harden again. Rolling it out immediately would produce a tough crust. When rolling the dough out, remember to use strong, swift movements, and as little flour as possible. The more the dough is poked and prodded, the more flakiness is sacrificed.

All of the pastry recipes in this chapter call for butter. Lard, vegetable shortening, goose fat, and many other fats can be used in place of butter. Butter produces a richer flavor, while lard and vegetable shortening produce a flakier crust. It is a matter of personal preference.

Basic Pastry

2 cups flour
⅔ cup butter or lard, cold
2 - 3 tablespoons ice water

Mix and sift flour and ¾ teaspoon salt. Cut in butter with knife or pulse in food processor. Add only water enough to hold ingredients together. Do not knead. Divide dough in 2 parts and wrap in plastic wrap. Refrigerate for at least 1 hour.

When ready to bake, preheat oven to 425°. Thinly roll out on a slightly floured board. Line pie pan with half pastry. Pinch pastry with fingers to make fancy edge and prick bottom and sides with fork. Bake for 10 to 15 minutes.

For 2-crust pie, line pie pan with pastry, put in filling, cover with top crust and bake as directed for pies. If a less rich pastry is desired, use only ½ cup butter. Yields 2 pastry shells.

Flaky Pastry

2 cups flour
⅔ cup butter, cold
Up to 2 tablespoons ice water or cider vinegar

Mix and sift flour and 1 teaspoon salt. Cut in 2 tablespoons butter with knife or pulse in food process or until butter is in pea-sized pieces.

Add enough water to make a stiff dough. Roll out in an oblong piece on slightly floured board and dot with bits of butter, using one-third remaining quantity.

Fold over ends to center and fold again to make 4 layers. Press ends together and roll out. Dot again with butter, fold and roll. Repeat this process a third time. Chill thoroughly. This pastry may be used whenever a basic pastry is called for. Yields 2 pastry shells.

Puff Paste

2 cups flour
1 cup butter, divided
Up to 2 tablespoons ice water or cider vinegar

Mix and sift flour and 1½ teaspoons salt. Cut in 2 tablespoons butter with knife or pulse in food processor until butter is in pea-sized pieces. Add just enough water to bind. Knead 5 minutes or pulse in food processor until it forms a ball. Cover. Refrigerate.

Roll on slightly floured board to ¼ inch thickness in rectangular shape with square corners. Slightly soften remaining butter and lay out in flat circular shape in center of dough. Fold other half over it. Press edges tightly together to hold in air.

Fold right side over and left side under enclosed butter. Refrigerate. Roll out again in rectangular shape. Fold ends toward center making 3 layers. Refrigerate.

Repeat this process 4 times. Refrigerate. Paste should be made at least 24 hours before baking and should be kept ice cold.

Hot Water Pastry

½ cup butter
1½ cups flour
¼ teaspoon baking powder

Cream butter in ¼ cup boiling water. Mix and sift flour, salt, and baking powder. Add dry mixture and ¾ teaspoon salt gradually to butter, blending well. Form into a ball and store in refrigerator until ready to use. Bake in 9-inch pie pan. Yields 1 pastry shell.

Tart Shells

Puff Paste:

2 cups flour
1 cup butter, divided
Up to 2 tablespoons ice water or cider vinegar

Mix and sift flour and 1½ teaspoons salt. Cut in 2 tablespoons butter with knife or pulse in food processor until butter is in pea-sized pieces. Add just enough water to bind. Knead 5 minutes or pulse in food processor until it forms a ball. Cover. Refrigerate.

Roll on slightly floured board to ¼ inch thickness in rectangular shape with square corners. Slightly soften remaining butter and lay out in flat circular shape in center of dough. Fold other half over it. Press edges tightly together to hold in air.

Fold right side over and left side under enclosed butter. Refrigerate. Roll out again in rectangular shape. Fold ends toward center making 3 layers. Refrigerate.

Repeat this process 4 times. Refrigerate. Paste should be made at least 24 hours before baking and should be kept ice cold.

When ready to bake, preehat oven to 375°. Roll out puff paste to ⅛ inch thickness. Cut into circles and fit over inverted pie, muffin or patty pans. Prick with fork. Bake for 25 to 20 minutes. Yields 2 tart shells.

While most recipes call for ingredients at room temperature, good pastry requires cold ingredients in order to produce a flaky crust. The butter or other shortening should be very cold. It can be helpful to refrigerate the flour before mixing as well.

Apple Pie

Basic Pastry (page 11)
6 cups peeled, cored apples, sliced ¼ inch thick
⅔ cup sugar
¼ teaspoon ground nutmeg
¼ teaspoon ground cinnamon
1 teaspoon lemon juice
2 teaspoons butter

Preheat oven to 375°. Lightly roll half of piecrust to ⅛ inch thickness and about 2½ inches larger than 9-inch pie pan. Fold it in half and fit it into pie pan.

In rolling piecrust use only enough flour to prevent sticking, handling the dough very lightly and never turning it.

Press piecrust lightly to fit pie pan and trim even with edge of pan, using a knife. Fill piecrust with apples.

Mix sugar, nutmeg, ⅛ teaspoon salt, cinnamon and lemon juice. Sprinkle over apples and dot with butter. Moisten edge of crust with cold water.

Roll other half of piecrust to ⅛ inch thickness and about 1 inch larger than the diameter of plate. Fold this in half and make 3 slits, each ½ inch length, in the center of the folded side. These will act as vents when the pie bakes.

Adjust over the filling, then carefully fold the edge of the upper crust under the lower crust all the way around. Finish by pressing edges together with fork dipped in flour.

If glazed surface is desired, brush top of pie with milk, cream or melted butter or slightly beaten egg white. Bake for 40 minutes. Serves 6.

One-Crust Apple Pie

4 large tart apples
½ cup sugar
Few grains ground nutmeg
½ teaspoon ground cinnamon
1 tablespoon butter
Basic Pastry (page 11)
Whipping cream, sweetened, whipped

Preheat oven to 375°. Wash, peel and core apples. Cut in thin slices. Place them in bottom of pie pan and sprinkle with sugar, nutmeg and cinnamon. Dot with small bits of butter.

Roll basic pastry thin and fit over the apples. Trim off edge of pastry and press with fingers or fork to make a fancy edge. Prick top to allow steam to escape.

Bake for 10 minutes. Reduce heat to 325° and bake for additional 20 minutes. Cool. Turn out upside down on serving dish. Cover with whipped cream. Serves 6.

In the 16th century, cookbooks began to include pastry recipes when cookbooks began to be published for household use rather than for the professional cook. Here is a recipe from a book published in 1545:

__To Make Short Paest for Tarte__ – Take fyne floure and a cursey of fayre water and a dysche of swete butter and a lyttel saffron, and the yolckes of two egges and make it thynne and as tender as ye maye.

Berry Pie

3 cups berries
1 cup sugar
2 tablespoons cornstarch or 4 tablespoons flour
1 tablespoon lemon juice
Basic Pastry (page 11)
1 tablespoon butter

Preheat oven to 375°. Mix fruit with combined sugar, cornstarch or flour, ⅛ teaspoon salt and lemon juice.

Roll pastry out to ⅛ inch thickness. Line pie pan with pastry. Fill with berries and dot with butter.

Moisten pastry edge and put top piecrust in place. The upper crust should be cut in several places so that steam can escape. Crimp edge and bake for about 10 minutes, reduce heat temperature to 325° for about 30 minutes to finish baking. Serves 6.

Fresh Strawberry Pie

6 cups ripe strawberries
¼ cup powdered sugar
Baked Basic Pastry (page 11)
Whipping cream, whipped

Wash and stem ripe strawberries. Roll them in powdered sugar and fill pastry shell. Top with whipped cream. Refrigerate. Serves 6.

Blueberry Pie

Basic Pastry (page 11)
3 - 4 cups fresh or frozen blueberries
⅔ - 1 cup sugar
¼ teaspoon ground nutmeg
¼ teaspoon ground cinnamon
1 teaspoon lemon juice
7 tablespoons tapioca
2 teaspoons butter

Preheat oven to 350°. Lightly roll half of piecrust to ⅛ inch thickness and about 2½ inches larger than 9-inch pie pan. Fold it in half and fit it into pie pan.

In rolling piecrust use only enough flour to prevent sticking, handling the dough very lightly and never turning it. Press piecrust lightly to fit pie pan and trim even with edge of pan, using a knife. Fill piecrust with blueberries.

Mix sugar, nutmeg, ⅛ teaspoon salt, cinnamon, lemon juice and tapioca in bowl. Sprinkle over blueberries and dot with butter. Moisten edge of crust with cold water.

Roll other half of piecrust to ⅛ inch thickness and about 1 inch larger than the diameter of plate. Fold this in half and make 3 slits, each ½ inch length, in the center of the folded side. These will act as vents when the pie bakes.

Adjust over the filling, then carefully fold the edge of the upper crust under the lower crust all the way around. Finish by pressing edges together with fork dipped in flour. If glazed surface is desired, brush top of pie with milk, cream, melted butter or slightly beaten egg white. Bake for 40 minutes. Serves 6.

TIP: Other fruits that can be used in berry pies include blackberries, plums, grapes, rhubarb or peaches.

Huckleberry Pie

Basic Pastry (page 11)
3 - 4 cups fresh or frozen huckleberries
⅔ - 1 cup sugar
¼ teaspoon ground nutmeg
¼ teaspoon ground cinnamon
1 teaspoon lemon juice
7 tablespoons tapioca
2 teaspoons butter

Preheat oven to 350°. Lightly roll half of piecrust to ⅛ inch thickness and about 2½ inches larger than 9-inch pie pan. Fold it in half and fit it into pie pan.

In rolling piecrust use only enough flour to prevent sticking, handling the dough very lightly and never turning it.

Press piecrust lightly to fit pie pan and trim even with edge of pan, using a knife. Fill piecrust with huckleberries.

Mix sugar, nutmeg, ⅛ teaspoon salt, cinnamon, lemon juice and tapioca in bowl. Sprinkle over huckleberries and dot with butter. Moisten edge of crust with cold water.

Roll other half of piecrust to ⅛ inch thickness and about 1 inch larger than the diameter of plate. Fold this in half and make 3 slits, each ½ inch length, in the center of the folded side. These will act as vents when the pie bakes.

Adjust over the filling, then carefully fold the edge of the upper crust under the lower crust all the way around. Finish by pressing edges together with fork dipped in flour.

If glazed surface is desired, brush top of pie with milk, cream or melted butter or slightly beaten egg white. Bake for 40 minutes. Serves 6.

Cherry Pie

Basic Pastry (page 11)
2½ cups canned cherries with liquid
Sugar

Preheat oven to 375°. Roll basic pastry out to ⅛ inch thickness. Line pie pan with pastry.

Drain cherries (save liquid) and place them on top of pastry. Sprinkle with sugar to taste. Pour over syrup from cherries. Top with layer of pastry. Wet edges of pastry.

Press together and trim. Cut crust in several places so that steam can escape. Bake for 10 minutes. Reduce heat to 325° and bake for additional 20 minutes. Serves 6.

Lattice Cherry Pie

Prepare cherry pie using recipes above. Make Basic Pastry (page 11) but instead of making solid piecrust, cut dough for 1 piecrust into ⅜ inch wide strips.

Crisscross strips of pastry over filling in 1 pie crust. Save 2 to 3 strips to put over ends of strips around edge to hold them in place. Serves 6.

Fruit pies do not freeze well after baking. If you freeze unbaked fruit pies, do not thaw them but bake from frozen at 425° for 15 or 20 minutes. Then lower the oven's temperature to the recommended level for the recipe and bake for the time specified in the recipe.

Peach Pie

8 peaches
½ cup sugar
Basic Pastry (page 11)
1 tablespoon butter

Preheat oven to 375°. Peel 8 peaches and slice thin. Simmer in ⅓ cup water for 10 minutes. Add sugar to taste.

Roll pastry out to ⅛ inch thickness on lightly floured board. Line pie pan with pastry and pour filling into it. Dot with small bits of butter.

Moisten edge of pastry, cover with a top crust and press edges together. Prick top with fork to allow steam to escape. Bake for 10 minutes. Reduce heat to 350° and bake 15 to 20 minutes. Serves 6.

Peach Pie Supreme

1 (3 ounce) package orange-flavored gelatin
1½ cups hot peach juice
2½ cups canned sliced peaches, drained
Baked Basic Pastry (page 11)

Dissolve gelatin in hot peach juice and 1½ cups water. Add peaches. Refrigerate. When slightly thickened, turn into cold baked piecrust. Refrigerate until firm. Serve with whipped cream, if desired. Serves 6.

> *Beginning with the early settlers and pioneers in America, pie was often served at every meal right up into the 20th century.*

Pumpkin Pie

Basic Pastry (page 11)
2 cups canned mashed pumpkin
1 cup milk
3 eggs, separated
½ cup sugar
1¼ teaspoons ground cinnamon
¼ teaspoon ground cloves
¼ teaspoon ground ginger
¼ teaspoon ground nutmeg

Preheat oven to 375°. Roll out pastry to ⅛ inch thickness on lightly floured board. Line pie pan with plain pastry and pinch with fingers to make fancy edge.

Mix pumpkin and milk in bowl. Add egg yolks. Add sugar mixed with cinnamon, cloves, ginger, nutmeg and 1 teaspoon salt. Mix well.

Stiffly beat egg whites. Fold them into pumpkin mixture. Turn into pie pan. Bake for 10 minutes, reduce heat to 325°, and bake for additional 20 minutes or until filling is firm. Serve with whipped cream, if desired. Serves 6.

The first "pies" were meat-filled pastries. The pastry was designed more as a container for the filling and was often inedible. They were called "coffyns" or "coffins", a word that meant basket then.

Rhubarb Pie

3 cups rhubarb
Basic Pastry (page 11)
1 cup sugar
2 tablespoons flour
2 eggs, beaten

Preheat oven to 375°. Peel rhubarb and cut in ½ inch pieces before measuring. Roll out pastry to ⅛ inch thickness on lightly floured board. Line pie pan with plain pastry.

Mix sugar, flour, ⅛ teaspoon salt and eggs in bowl. Add to rhubarb and turn into pie pan. Moisten edge of pastry with water. Cover with top crust.

Press edges together and trim. Gash top to let steam escape. Bake for 10 minutes. Reduce heat to 325° and continue baking for additional 30 minutes. Swerves 6.

Strawberry Chiffon Pie

1½ tablespoons unflavored gelatin
½ cup sugar
1 cup crushed strawberries
1 egg white, stiffly beaten
1 cup cream, whipped
Baked Basic Pastry (page 11)

Soak gelatin in ¼ cup cold water for 5 minutes. Dissolve in double boiler over hot water. Sprinkle sugar on berries and let stand until sugar dissolves. Add gelatin and ⅛ teaspoon salt, mixing well. Refrigerate.

When congealing starts, beat until light. Fold in egg white and whipped cream. Pile into baked piecrust. Refrigerate. Serves 6.

Lemon Meringue Pie

1½ tablespoons butter
½ cup flour
1 cup sugar
2 eggs, separated
Juice and peel of 1 lemon
Baked Basic Pastry (page 11)
2 tablespoons powdered sugar

Preheat oven to 325°. Melt butter in double boiler. Add flour, sugar, ¼ teaspoon salt, 2 cups water and egg yolks. Mix well. Cook until thick, stirring constantly.

Remove from heat, add lemon juice and peel, and mix well. Pour into baked piecrust. Cover top with Meringue (page 98) made by beating powdered sugar into stiffly beaten egg whites. Bake until a delicate brown for about 15 minutes. The filling may also be used for lemon tarts. Serves 6.

Lemon Chiffon Pie

½ tablespoon gelatin
4 eggs, separated
1 cup sugar, divided
Juice and peel of 1 lemon
Baked Basic Pastry (page 11)
1 cup cream, whipped

Soak gelatin in 2 tablespoons cold water for 5 minutes. Dissolve in double boiler. Mix yolks, ½ teaspoon salt, ½ cup sugar, lemon juice and peel in double boiler. Cook, stirring constantly until thick. Add gelatin and cook for additional 1 minute. Beat egg whites to peaks with remaining sugar. Gently fold liquid mixture into egg whites. Turn into baked piecrust. Top with whipped cream. Cool. Serves 6.

Cream Pie

1 tablespoon butter
¼ cup flour
⅔ cup sugar
2 cups milk
2 eggs, separated
1 teaspoon vanilla
Baked Basic Pastry (page 11)
2 tablespoons powdered sugar

Preheat oven to 325°. Melt butter in double boiler. Add flour, sugar, ¼ teaspoon salt, milk, and egg yolks and cook in until thick, stirring constantly. Add vanilla. Pour into piecrust.

Cover top with meringue made by beating powdered sugar into stiffly beaten egg whites. Bake for 15 minutes or until delicate brown. Serves 6.

One baking step that cannot be done ahead of time is beating egg whites. After 5 minutes they will begin to lose volume. Egg whites will whip better when at room temperature because the protein in the eggs is more elastic and will whip up into more of the tiny air bubbles. If the eggs are colder, they will take longer to beat. Unfortunately, in high humidity, you sometimes will not be able to get the correct volume no matter what.

Banana Cream Pie

1 tablespoon butter
¼ cup flour
⅔ cup sugar
2 cups milk
2 eggs, separated
1 teaspoon vanilla
Baked Basic Pastry (page 11)
1 banana
2 tablespoons powdered sugar

Preheat oven to 325°. Melt butter in double boiler. Add flour, sugar, ¼ teaspoon salt, milk, and egg yolks and cook until thick, stirring constantly. Add vanilla. Pour into piecrust. Slice banana thinly and arrange over filling.

Cover top with meringue made by beating powdered sugar into stiffly beaten egg whites. Bake for 15 minutes or until delicate brown. Serves 6.

Boston Cream Pie

3 tablespoons sugar
2 cups milk, divided
2 tablespoons cornstarch
1 egg, beaten
1 tablespoon vanilla
2 Washington Pie layers (page 38)
1 tablespoon powdered sugar

Dissolve sugar in 1½ cups milk in bowl. In separate bowl, combine cornstarch with remaining milk. Combine mixtures. Add egg. Cook slowly, stirring constantly until thick. Add vanilla. Spread filling between Washington Pie layers. Sprinkle powdered sugar on top. Serves 6.

Banana-Fruit Chiffon Pie

1 cup mashed ripe bananas
2 tablespoons lemon juice
½ cup orange juice
¼ teaspoon grated lemon peel
¼ teaspoon grated orange peel
½ cup sugar
3 eggs, separated
1 tablespoon unflavored gelatin
Baked Basic Pastry (page 11)

Mix bananas, juices, peels, ⅓ teaspoon salt, sugar and egg yolks in bowl. Cook in double boiler until mixture has thickened. Stir in gelatin which has been soaked for 5 minutes in ⅓ cup cold water and stir until dissolved. Cool. Stiffly beat egg whites. Gently fold in whites and pour into piecrust. Refrigerate until firm. Serves 6.

Chess Pie

Puff Paste (page 12)
⅓ cup butter
½ cup sugar
3 egg yolks, well beaten
½ teaspoon vanilla
Meringue (page 98)

Roll puff paste out to ¼ inch thickness on lightly floured board. Line pie pan with puff paste. Refrigerate.

When ready to bake, preheat oven to 350°. Cream butter and sugar. Add yolks and vanilla. Turn into pie pan. Bake until very light for about 30 minutes. Top with meringue. Bake again for 12 minutes. Cut in wedges to serve while hot. Serves 6.

Chocolate Pie

Basic Pastry (page 11)
2 ounces dark chocolate
1 cup sugar
2 tablespoons flour
3 eggs, well beaten
½ cup chopped nuts, optional
1 cup cream, whipped

Preheat oven to 375°. Roll out pastry to ⅛ inch thickness on lightly floured board. Line pie pan with pastry. Pinch edge with fingers to make fancy.

Shave chocolate and melt in double boiler. Add sugar, flour and chocolate to eggs. Beat thoroughly. Turn into pie pan.

Bake for 20 minutes or until set. Refrigerate. Sprinkle with nuts, if desired. Top with whipped cream. Garnish, if desired with half cherries and whole nuts. Serves 6.

When placing a bottom crust in a pie pan, gently ease the piecrust into the pan without stretching it. Carefully tuck the crust into the crease around the bottom of the pan.

Chocolate Chiffon Pie

¾ cup sugar, divided
4 eggs, separated
⅓ cup milk
2 ounces dark chocolate
½ tablespoon gelatin
1 teaspoon vanilla
Baked Basic Pastry (page 11)

Beat 6 tablespoons sugar into egg yolks. Cook in double boiler, stirring constantly until thickened. Bring milk to boiling pointin saucepan and shave in chocolate. Blend thoroughly.

Soak gelatin in 1 tablespoon cold water for 5 minutes. Dissolve in milk-chocolate mixture. Add vanilla and ¼ teaspoon salt and pour milk mixture into egg mixture. Mix well and refrigerate.

Beat egg whites with remaining sugar until stiff. Fold gently into chilled chocolate mixture. Turn into piecrust. Refrigerate. Serves 6.

When beating egg whites, be sure the bowl is spotless and grease-free; metal bowls seem to work better than plastic. Even a tiny speck of fat or egg yolk can cause whipped egg whites to have less volume.

Chocolate Cream Pie

2 tablespoons butter
6 tablespoons flour
1½ cups milk
2 ounces dark chocolate, shaved
¾ cup sugar
2 eggs, separated
1 teaspoon vanilla
Baked Basic Pastry (page 11)
2 tablespoons powdered sugar

Preheat oven to 325°. Melt butter in saucepan and add flour, milk, chocolate, sugar and ¼ teaspoon salt. Heat slowly to boiling point, stirring constantly, until thick and smooth. Remove from heat. Add egg yolks and vanilla. Turn into piecrust.

Beat powdered sugar into egg whites until stiff peaks form. Top pie with meringue. Bake until delicate brown for about 15 minutes.

Whipped cream may be substituted for meringue, but it should be added after the pie has cooled. Serves 6.

When cutting a pie with a meringue, dip your knife blade in a tall glass of very hot water before every cut. Cutting the pie will be much smoother. This method also works with cakes.

Coconut Cream Pie

⅓ cup sugar
2 tablespoons cornstarch
3 egg yolks
1½ cups scalded milk
1 tablespoon butter
½ cup shredded coconut
½ teaspoon vanilla
Baked Basic Pastry (page 11)

Preheat oven to 325°. Add sugar, cornstarch, and ¼ teaspoon salt to egg yolks in bowl. Add scalded milk, and cook in double boiler, stirring until thickened. Add butter, coconut and vanilla.

Pour into a pie pan lined with basic pastry. Bake for 15 minutes, or until filling has set. The pie may be covered with Meringue (page 98). Serves 6.

TIP: *To scald milk, bring milk just to a boil and remove from heat. Cool slightly before using.*

Why are pie pans round? Colonial housewives literally cut corners to stretch the ingredients. This is also why pie pans are shallow.

Custard Pie

Basic Pastry (page 11)
¾ cup sugar
4 tablespoons flour
3 tablespoons butter, softened
3 cups milk
3 eggs, slightly beaten
1 teaspoon vanilla

Preheat oven to 350°. Roll piecrust to ⅛ inch thickness and 2 inches larger than diameter of plate. Line 9-inch pie pan with piecrust, fitting it loosely.

Fold back edge of piecrust all the way round and bring this double fold to an upright position. Flute double fold of piecrust in the following manner: Place floured tip or knuckle of index finger of right hand against the fold on the inside of the piecrust rim. Pinch gently, then remove the fingers and continue this same fluting motion around the entire rim of the pie.

Combine sugar, flour and ½ teaspoon salt in bowl, cut in butter and stir until mixture is like coarse crumbs. Add milk, eggs and vanilla and beat. Pour in piecrust. Bake for 30 to 40 minutes or until knife inserted in center comes out clean. Serves 6.

Favorite pie recipes were brought primarily from England as America was colonized. Immigrants adapted to ingredients available in the New World.

Caramel Custard Pie

Basic Pastry (page 11)
¾ cup packed brown sugar
4 tablespoons flour
3 tablespoons butter, softened
3 cups milk
3 eggs, slightly beaten
1 teaspoon vanilla

Preheat oven to 350°. Roll piecrust to ⅛ inch thickness and 2 inches larger than diameter of plate. Line 9-inch pie pan with piecrust, fitting it loosely.

Fold back edge of piecrust all the way round and bring this double fold to an upright position. Flute double fold of piecrust in the following manner: Place floured tip or knuckle of index finger of right hand against the fold on the inside of the piecrust rim. Pinch gently, then remove the fingers and continue this same fluting motion around the entire rim of the pie.

Combine brown sugar, flour and ½ teaspoon salt in bowl, cut in butter and stir until mixture is like coarse crumbs. Add milk, eggs and vanilla and beat. Pour into piecrust. Bake for 30 to 40 minutes or until knife inserted in center comes out clean. Serves 6.

Many people prefer to bake pies in glass pie pans because they can check the browning of the crust on the bottom. Most recommend that the oven temperature be reduced by 25° when using glass.

Coconut Custard Pie

Basic Pastry (page 11)
¾ **cup sugar**
4 **tablespoons flour**
3 **tablespoons butter, softened**
¼ **cup shredded coconut**
3 **cups milk**
3 **eggs, slightly beaten**
1 **teaspoon vanilla**

Preheat oven to 350°. Roll piecrust to ⅛ inch thickness and 2 inches larger than diameter of plate. Line 9-inch pie pan with piecrust, fitting it loosely.

Fold back edge of piecrust all the way round and bring this double fold to an upright position. Flute double fold of piecrust in the following manner: Place floured tip or knuckle of index finger of right hand against the fold on the inside of the piecrust rim. Pinch gently, then remove the fingers and continue this same fluting motion around the entire rim of the pie.

Combine sugar, flour and ½ teaspoon salt in bowl, cut in butter and stir until mixture is like coarse crumbs. Add coconut with milk, eggs and vanilla and beat. Pour in piecrust. Bake for 30 to 40 minutes or until silver knife inserted in center comes out clean. Serves 6.

It's a good idea to refrigerate pastry for 30 or 40 minutes before rolling it out. Pastry that is well wrapped can be refrigerated for 2 or 3 days. If the pastry is refrigerated longer than 30 or 40 minutes, let it stand at room temperature for 5 or 10 minutes before rolling it out.

Lemon Custard Pie

Basic Pastry (page 11)
¾ **cup sugar**
4 tablespoons flour
3 tablespoons butter, softened
3 cups milk
3 eggs, slightly beaten
2 lemon peels, grated

Preheat oven to 350°. Roll piecrust to ⅛ inch thickness and 2 inches larger than diameter of plate. Line 9-inch pie pan with piecrust, fitting it loosely.

Fold back edge of piecrust all the way round and bring this double fold to an upright position. Flute double fold of piecrust in the following manner: Place floured tip or knuckle of index finger of right hand against the fold on the inside of the piecrust rim. Pinch gently, then remove the fingers and continue this same fluting motion around the entire rim of the pie.

Combine sugar, flour and ½ teaspoon salt in bowl, cut in butter and stir until mixture is like coarse crumbs. Add milk, eggs and lemon rind and beat. Pour in piecrust. Bake for 30 to 40 minutes or until knife inserted in center comes out clean. Serves 6.

Zest is the finely grated colored outside of lemon or orange peel. Be careful not to grate the white part on the inside of the peel because it is bitter.

Eggnog Pie

1 tablespoon granulated unflavored gelatin
2 eggs, well beaten
3 tablespoons powdered sugar
1 cup whipping cream, whipped
2 tablespoons whisky or 1 teaspoon vanilla
Baked Basic Pastry (page 11)
Ground nutmeg

Soften gelatin in ¼ cup cold water. Dissolve in 1 cup boiling water. Refrigerate until slightly thickened. Beat with hand mixer until fluffy.

Beat eggs well. Add ¼ teaspoon salt. Beat in powdered sugar. Fold into gelatin. Fold in cream. Add whisky or vanilla. Refrigerate again until thickened.

Turn into baked piecrust and refrigerate until firm at least 1 hour. Garnish with additional whipped cream and nutmeg, if desired. Serves 6.

When eggs are called for in baking, use large eggs. Most recipes are based on large eggs.

Molasses Pie

1 cup molasses
1 tablespoon flour
1 lemon
Basic Pastry (page 11)

Preheat oven to 350°. Beat molasses and flour in bowl. Zest and squeeze lemon and add juice, pulp and zest to molasses. Line pie pan with pastry. Turn in mixture.

Make top crust with layer of pastry. Wet edges of pastry with water. Press together and trim. Bake for 10 minutes. Reduce heat and continue baking at 325° for 20 minutes. Serves 6.

Pecan Pie

3 eggs
½ cup sugar
1 cup corn syrup
1 teaspoon vanilla
¼ cup butter, melted
Basic Pastry (page 11)
1 cup pecans

Preheat oven to 350°. Beat eggs in bowl. Add sugar, syrup, ⅛ teaspoon salt, vanilla and butter. Roll pastry out to ⅛ inch thickness on lightly floured board. Line pie pan with plain pastry.

Place pecans in a layer. Add mixture. Bake for 50 to 60 minutes. The nuts will rise to top and form a crusted layer. Serves 6.

Always cut slits in the top crust of a pie to release the steam as the pie bakes. Otherwise, the top may burst open on top or at the edges.

Sweet Potato Pecan Pie

¼ cup butter at room temperature
½ cup packed brown sugar
1 cup mashed boiled sweet potatoes
3 eggs
⅓ cup corn syrup
⅓ cup milk
1 teaspoon vanilla
1 cup broken pecans
Basic Pastry (page 11)

Preheat oven to 375°. Cream butter and brown sugar in bowl. Add sweet potatoes and slightly beaten eggs. Beat well. Combine with syrup, milk, ½ teaspoon salt, vanilla and pecans.

Roll pastry out to ⅛ inch thickness on lightly floured board. Line pie pan with plain pastry. Turn mixture into pan. Bake for 10 minutes. Reduce heat to 325° and continue baking for additional 35 to 45 minutes. Serve with whipped cream, if desired. Serves 6.

When making pastry (piecrust), cut the fat into the flour until the mixture is a crumbly texture about the size of small peas. If the mixture is more thoroughly mixed, the crust will be less flaky.

Washington Pie

⅓ cup butter at room temperature
1 cup sugar, divided
2 eggs, well beaten
1¾ cups flour
2 teaspoons baking powder
½ cup milk
½ teaspoon vanilla
½ cup raspberry jam
2 tablespoons powdered sugar

Preheat oven to 375°. Cream butter in bowl. Add half sugar gradually. Beat until light. Add remaining sugar to eggs and beat. Combine mixtures.

In separate bowl, mix and sift flour, baking powder and ½ teaspoon salt and add alternately with milk to first mixture. Beat thoroughly and
add vanilla.

Bake in 2 sprayed 8-inch layer cake pans for 20 to 30 minutes. Use raspberry jam between layers and sprinkle top with powdered sugar. Serves 6 to 8.

Always stir flour before measuring, then spoon it into a measuring cup and level the top with a knife. Do not shake down the flour or pack it. If you scoop the flour with the cup, it may settle and cause you to have more flour than the recipe calls for.

The Pie Lady's Piecrust

1 cup flour
½ cup shortening

Preheat oven to 350°. Mix flour and shortening in bowl. Add ½ cup cold water and ½ teaspoon salt. Form a ball and roll into 1 piecrust. Bake until brown.

The Pie Lady's Chocolate Cream Pie

2 cups plus 2 tablespoons sugar, divided
½ cup flour
2 tablespoons cocoa
3 eggs, separated
1 (12 ounce) can evaporated milk
2 tablespoons butter
2 teaspoons vanilla, divided
1 (10 inch) baked piecrust or Basic Pastry (page 11)

Mix 1½ cups sugar, flour and cocoa in heavy saucepan and set aside.

Beat 3 egg yolks in bowl and combine with ½ cup sugar, evaporated milk and ½ teaspoon salt in bowl. Pour into saucepan with sugar, flour and cocoa. Cook over medium heat, stirring occasionally, until mixture thickens. Add up to 1 cup hot water to mixture as it cooks to keep it from getting too thick. Remove from heat and add butter and 1 teaspoon vanilla and stir until smooth. Pour into piecrust.

To make meringue, beat 3 egg whites in bowl until soft peaks form. Gradually add 2 tablespoons sugar and 1 teaspoon vanilla and beat until stiff peaks form. Spread meringue over pie filling and brown slightly at 350° for 15 to 20 minutes. Serves 6.

EthelLene Oliver (See pages 5 and 6 for her story.)

The Pie Lady's Caramel Pie

1½ cups plus ⅔ cup plus 2 tablespoons sugar, divided
3 eggs, separated
½ cup flour
1 (12 ounce) can evaporated milk
1 (10 inch) baked piecrust or Basic Pastry (page 11)
1 teaspoon vanilla

Melt 1½ cups sugar in heavy pan, add 1½ cups water and boil until smooth. Beat 3 egg yolks in bowl and combine with ⅔ cup sugar, flour, evaporated milk and 1 teaspoon salt. Cook until mixture thickens. Add up to 1 cup hot water to mixture as it cooks to keep it from getting to thick. Mix well and pour into piecrust.

To make merignue, beat egg whites in bowl until soft peaks form. Gradually add 2 tablespoons sugar and vanilla and beat until stiff peaks form. Spread meringue over pie filling and brown slightly at 350° for 15 to 20 minutes. Serves 6.

The Pie Lady's Pecan Pie

3 eggs
1 cup sugar
1 cup white corn syrup
1½ cups pecan halves
1 tablespoon butter
1 teaspoon vanilla
1 (10 inch) piecrust or Basic Pastry (page 11)

Preheat oven to 300°. Mix all ingredients in bowl and pour into unbaked piecrust and bake for 1 hour. Serves 6.

EthelLene Oliver (See pages 5 and 6 for her story.)

The Pie Lady's Coconut Cream Pie

2 cups plus 2 tablespoons sugar, divided
½ cup flour
3 eggs, separated
1 (12 ounce) can evaporated milk
2 tablespoons butter
2 teaspoons vanilla, separated
1⅓ cups shredded coconut
1 (10 inch) baked piecrust or Basic Pastry (page 11)

Mix 1½ cups sugar and flour in heavy saucepan and set aside.

Beat 3 egg yolks in bowl and combine with ½ cup sugar and evaporated milk.

Pour into saucepan with sugar-flour mixture and cook over medium heat, stirring occasionally, until mixture thickens. Add up to 1 cup water to mixture as it cooks to keep it from getting to thick.

Remove from heat and add butter, 1 teaspoon vanilla and 1 cup shredded coconut. Pour into piecrust

To make merignue, beat 3 egg whites in bowl until soft peaks form. Gradually add 2 tablespoons sugar and about 1 teaspoon vanilla and beat until stiff peaks form. Spread meringue over pie, and sprinkle a little coconut over top and brown slightly at 350° for about 15 to 20 minutes. Serves 6.

EthelLene Oliver (See pages 5 and 6 for her story.)

Fried Pies

2 cups flour
½ cup butter or lard, cold
2 - 3 tablespoons ice water
Applesauce
Canola oil
Powdered sugar

Mix and sift flour and ¾ teaspoon salt in bowl. Cut in butter with knife or pulse in food processor.

Add only enough water to hold ingredients together. Do not knead. Divide dough in 2 parts and wrap in plastic wrap. Refrigerate for at least 1 hour.

When ready to bake, roll out pastry to ⅛ inch thickness. Cut in large circles, 3½ inches to 4 inches across. Put 1 tablespoon of applesauce in center of pastry. Moisten edges with cold water.

Fold over so as to make a semi-circle. Press edges together with tines of fork. Fry in deep hot oil (375°) until delicate brown. Drain on unglazed paper. Sprinkle with powdered sugar and serve warm. Serves 8 to 10.

What's the difference between powdered sugar and confectioner's sugar? Confectioner's sugar is the finest grade of powdered sugar. Powdered sugars have been used since the 18th century and cake frosting became popular with this development.

Cherry Tarts

2½ cups canned red cherries
1 tablespoon cornstarch
½ cup sugar
6 baked Tart Shells (page 13)

Drain juice from cherries. Combine cherry juice, 1 cup boiling water and sugar in saucepan. Bring to boiling point and strain. Make smooth paste of cornstarch and a little cold water. Add to hot syrup, stirring constantly.

Cook, still stirring, over medium heat until mixture thickens. While hot pour over cherries. Let filling cool before filling tart shells. Serve with whipped cream. Yields 6 tarts.

TIP: *Sliced or chopped canned peaches, pineapple, apricots, strawberries, loganberries, raspberries, Royal Anne cherries, blackberries, blueberries or cranberries may be substituted for the red sour pitted cherries in the recipe.*

Centuries ago, enormous pies were made. A favorite savory pie of Emperor William I of Germany when he visited Queen Victoria contained a whole turkey stuffed with a chicken stuffed with a pheasant stuffed with a woodcock.

Lemon Tarts

1½ cups sugar plus 6 tablespoons
½ cup flour
2 tablespoons cornstarch
3 eggs, separated
6 tablespoons lemon juice (2 - 3 lemons)
2 tablespoons grated lemon peel
12 baked Tart Shells (page 13)

Combine 1½ cups sugar, flour, cornstarch, and ½ teaspoon salt in bowl. Add 2¼ cups boiling water gradually, stirring constantly. Beat egg yolks and pour hot mixture over them, stirring constantly. Cook slowly for 5 minutes.

Add lemon juice and peel. Mix well. Cool. Pour into tart shells. Cover with meringue made by beating egg whites stiffly with remaining sugar. Yields 12 tarts.

Orange-Rhubarb Tarts

2 pounds rhubarb, cut into small pieces
1½ cups sugar
2 oranges, peeled, seeded, membranes removed
1 tablespoon unflavored gelatin
12 baked Tart Shells (page 13)
Whipped cream

Preheat oven to 350°. Combine rhubarb with sugar and orange segments cut in small pieces in bowl. Put mixture in sprayed baking dish. Bake for 50 to 60 minutes.

Soak gelatin in 2 tablespoons cold water and then dissolve in double boiler. Stir into cooked fruit. Cool. Fill tart shells with chilled mixture and top with whipped cream. Yields 12 tarts.

Pumpkin Tarts

Basic Pastry (page 11)
2½ cups mashed canned pumpkin
2 cups packed brown sugar
4 eggs, slightly beaten
1 cup milk
2 tablespoons melted butter
1 tablespoon molasses
1 teaspoon ground cinnamon
¾ teaspoon ground ginger
½ teaspoon ground nutmeg
Whipped cream

Preheat oven to 375°. Roll pastry out to ⅛ inch thickness on lightly floured board. Cut dough in circles that are slightly larger than tart cups. Repeat as necessary to get 6 crusts. Line 6 tart cups with plain pastry.

Mix remaining ingredients and ½ teaspoon salt in bowl. Beat well. Pile in tart shells. Bake for 40 minutes. Serve hot or cold. If cold, top with layer of whipped cream. Serves 6.

Baking is a method of applying dry heat to food in an enclosed space – like an oven.

Strawberry Tartlets

½ cup sugar
2 tablespoons flour
2 eggs, well beaten
1 cup milk, scalded
½ teaspoon vanilla
½ cup whipping cream, whipped
Basic Pastry (page 11)
3 cups washed strawberries
¾ cup currant jelly

Preheat oven to 350°. Combine sugar, ¼ teaspoon salt, flour and eggs in saucepan, mixing well. Add milk slowly. Cook slowly over low heat, stirring constantly, until thick. Add vanilla. Fold in cream. Roll piecrust to ⅛ inch thickness.

Cut into rounds with 4 or 5-inch cookie cutter. Fit rounds over bottom of large muffin pan and trim. Prick entire surface of each with fork. Bake for 12 to 15 minutes. Remove from oven. Cool.

Lift from pans. Invert on cake rack. Fill shells half full of milk-egg mixture. Put layer of strawberries in tarts. Heat jelly until it melts and put 1 tablespoon over each tart. Yields 12 tarts.

TIP: To scald milk, bring milk just to a boil and remove from heat. Cool slightly before using.

Read recipes carefully before beginning to be sure you have the ingredients, the pans and any other equipment, and you have enough preparation and baking time to make the recipe.

Apple Turnovers

Basic Pastry (page 11)
4 apples, peeled, cored, thinly sliced
½ cup sugar
1 teaspoon ground cinnamon
2 tablespoons butter

Preheat oven to 350°. Roll out dough into rounds about the size of large saucer about 6 inches across. On half round arrange thin slices of apple. Sprinkle with sugar and cinnamon. Dot with butter.

Moisten rim of pastry with water. Fold over uncovered half of pastry and press edges together with fork. Prick top. Bake until apples are tender, about 20 minutes. Serves 6.

Cherry Turnovers

Basic Pastry (page 11)
¾ - 1 pound Bing cherries, pitted, halved
½ cup sugar
2 tablespoons butter

Preheat oven to 350°. Roll out dough into rounds about the size of large saucer about 6 inches across. On half round arrange cherries. Sprinkle with sugar and dot with butter.

Moisten rim of pastry with water. Fold over uncovered half of pastry and press edges together with fork. Prick top. Bake until apples are tender, about 20 minutes. Serbes 6 to 8.

Butterscotch Stacks

Basic Pastry (page 11)
3 tablespoons butter
1½ cups packed brown sugar
3 egg yolks
1½ cups milk
6 tablespoons flour
Whipped cream

Preheat oven to 350°. Roll pastry to about ⅛ inch thickness and cut into 3-inch rounds with cookie cutter. Place on baking sheet and bake for about 10 minutes. Cool.

Melt butter in small saucepan over low heat, add brown sugar, allow to brown slightly, then gradually add ¾ cup boiling water.

Beat egg yolks in bowl. Add 2 tablespoons of milk and flour, and beat until smooth. Add remainder of milk and ⅜ teaspoon salt. Pour this slowly into brown sugar mixture and cook over medium heat until thick, stirring constantly.

Cool and place 1 spoonful on top of each pastry round. Stack these in threes and top with whipped cream. Serves 4.

I left my butter in the freezer; now what? Grate it and let it stand for about a minute and it's ready to use. It will warm quickly as you work with it.

Cakes
&
Frostings

Cakes create warm memories
for every special occasion!

Cakes & Frostings Contents

Cakes

Cakes come in two major types: foam and buttered. Foam cakes, such as angel food cake and sponge cake, contain no butter or shortening. They get all of their volume from stiffly beaten egg whites. As a result, they have a light, spongy texture. The egg whites for these cakes should be beaten just until stiff. Overbeaten egg whites will become grainy and lose some of their volume, resulting in a heavier cake.

Care should be taken to fold in the egg whites with the rest of the batter as gently as possible, so as to maximize their effect. Mixing the egg whites in by hand, rather than with a mixer, will provide the best results.

Most cakes are buttered. They contain a combination of eggs, flour, and butter or shortening. The recipes in this book all call for butter. Shortening may be substituted in any of the recipes. Butter provides a richer taste, but shortening can sometimes provide a superior texture. Using butter or shortening is a matter of personal preference.

Most buttered cakes use a creaming method. For the creaming method, all of the ingredients for the cake should be at room temperature. (If using cold butter just microwave it for a few seconds, making sure the butter is softened, but not hot.) The butter and sugar are creamed together, and the eggs are added one at a time, and beaten until they are fully incorporated. This butter-sugar-egg mixture should be beaten thoroughly. This not only makes a uniform mixture, but also incorporates air into the batter.

The flour should be sifted with the other dry ingredients, and then added to the butter mixture. This should be done as swiftly as possible. The batter should only be beaten until the flour is incorporated. Mixing beyond that point can result in a tougher cake.

Whether making a foam cake or a buttered cake, the oven should be preheated to the correct temperature and the cake pans should be ready and waiting. Once the batter is ready, it should go in the oven as quickly as possible. Try not to disturb the cake for the first 15 or 20 minutes of baking. Opening and closing the door too many times can cause the cake to fall.

The easiest way to test a cake for doneness is to stick a knife or toothpick into the cake. If it comes out clean, the cake is done.

Cakes should be allowed to cool for a few minutes after they have been removed from the oven. They should then be moved to a cooling rack. Doing this too soon can result in a broken cake. The cake should be completely cooled before it is frosted.

Angel Food Cake

1 cup sifted flour
1 - 1¼ cups sugar
8 egg whites
¾ teaspoon cream of tartar
1 teaspoon vanilla

Preheat oven to 325°. Sift flour and half sugar in bowl several times. Beat egg whites with ½ teaspoon salt until frothy.

Add cream of tartar and beat until whites start to peak. Gently fold in remaining sugar.

Then fold in flour-sugar mixture gradually and gently and when whole is partly blended add vanilla. Only gentle folding motion should be used in mixing, for stirring releases the air depended on for leavening.

A tube pan is best for baking angel food. Bake for about 1 hour. After baking, invert the cake and remove from pan when almost cold. Serves 18.

To split cake layers horizontally, loop unflavored dental floss around the cake, cross the ends and slowly pull on each end to cut through the layer.

Apple Upside-Down Cake

¼ cup butter at room temperature
½ cup sugar
1 egg
1 teaspoon vanilla
1½ cups sifted flour
2 teaspoons baking powder
2 - 4 firm-fleshed apples, such as Granny Smith
½ cup milk
2 teaspoons ground cinnamon mixed with ¼ cup sugar
Whipped cream

Preheat oven to 350°. Cream butter and sugar in bowl. Beat in egg and vanilla. In separate bowl, sift dry ingredients and ¼ teaspoon salt and alternately add it and milk to first mixture.

Spread thick coating of butter on bottom and sides of a 9 x 9-inch glass baking dish or very heavy pan. Peel, quarter and slice apples thin. Spread in an overlapping layer on bottom of baking dish and sprinkle with cinnamon and sugar.

Pour cake mixture over apples. The batter is rather thick and may need to be smoothed on top with knife. Bake for 45 minutes.

Loosen sides of cake, turn it carefully upside down and top will be covered with neat layer of transparent apples. Serve with whipped cream. Serves 9.

The Industrial Revolution with its introduction of mass production along with the transportation provided by railroads made ingredients for baking more available and affordable.

Pineapple Upside-Down Cake

¼ cup butter at room temperature
½ cup sugar
1 egg
1 teaspoon vanilla
1½ cups sifted flour
2 teaspoons baking powder
½ medium pineapple, peeled, cored, cubed
½ cup milk
Whipped cream

Preheat oven to 350°. Cream butter and sugar in bowl. Beat in egg and vanilla. In separate bowl, sift dry ingredients and ¼ teaspoon salt and alternately add it and milk to first mixture.

Spread thick coating of butter on bottom and sides of a 9 x 9-inch glass baking dish or very heavy pan. Spread pineapple chunks in an overlapping layer on bottom of baking dish and sprinkle with additional sugar.

Pour cake mixture over pineapple. The batter is rather thick and may need to be smoothed on top with knife. Bake for 45 minutes.

Loosen sides of cake, turn it carefully upside down and top will be covered with neat layer of transparent apples. Serve with whipped cream. Serves 9.

Centuries ago cakes were only baked for very special occasions or for the wealthy because the ingredients were so expensive. To this day, we think of cakes when celebrating an anniversary, wedding or birthday.

Applesauce Cake

½ cup butter at room temperature
1½ cups packed brown sugar
1 egg
1 teaspoon baking soda
1 cup thick applesauce
1 teaspoon ground cinnamon
½ teaspoon ground clove
1½ - 2 cups flour
1 cup raisins (optional)

Preheat oven to 350°. Cream butter, brown sugar and egg in bowl. Dissolve baking soda in applesauce and add to egg mixture.

Sift 1 teaspoon salt, cinnamon and clove with part of flour and add to first mixture. Add enough flour to make fairly stiff batter.

Add raisins, if desired. Pour into sprayed loaf pan and bake for 50 to 60 minutes until toothpick inserted in center comes out clean. Serves 10 to 12.

Cakes should be cooled in pans for about 10 to 15 minutes before turning out on a wire rack to cool. Put a couple of paper towels on the rack to keep the wires from leaving an imprint on the cake or breaking the top of the cake.

Birthday Cake

½ cup butter
1½ cups sugar
3 eggs
2¼ cups flour
3 teaspoons baking powder
⅔ cup milk
1 teaspoon almond extract

Preheat oven to 350°. Cream butter, sugar and eggs in bowl. In separate, bowl, mix and sift flour, 1 teaspoon salt and baking powder. Alternately add flour mixture and milk to first mixture. Add almond extract and beat thoroughly.

Pour into sprayed tube pan. Bake for 50 to 60 minutes or until toothpick inserted in center comes out clean. Cover and decorate with Ornamental Frosting (page 95) and sprinkles. Serves 18.

Crumb Cake

½ cup butter, chilled
1½ cups packed brown sugar
2½ cups sifted flour, divided
2½ teaspoons baking powder
1 teaspoon ground cinnamon
1 egg, beaten
¾ cup milk

Preheat oven to 375°. Mix butter, brown sugar and 2 cups flour in bowl to a fine crumb. Reserve ¾ cup of crumb. In separate bowl, sift remaining flour, baking powder, cinnamon and 1 teaspoon salt. Combine with remaining crumb mixture. Add egg and milk and mix well.

Pour into an 8-inch square pan that has been lined with parchment paper. Sprinkle reserved crumbs on top. Bake for 35 to 40 minutes or until toothpick inserted in center comes out clean. Serves 9.

Date Cake

4 eggs, separated
1½ cups packed brown sugar
⅔ cup butter at room temperature
3¼ cups flour
5 teaspoons baking powder
1 teaspoon ground cinnamon
½ teaspoon ground nutmeg
¾ cup milk
1½ cups chopped dates

Preheat oven to 350°. Separate eggs. Cream yolks, brown sugar and butter in bowl. In separate bowl, mix and sift flour, baking powder, 1 teaspoon salt, cinnamon, and nutmeg. Add dry mixture to first mixture alternately with milk.

Beat egg whites well, until they form peaks. Stir into mixture. Add dates, mixing well. Turn into sprayed tube pan. Bake for 50 to 60 minutes. Cool and frost as desired. Serves 18.

Tossing fruit or nuts in flour until coated will help them stay in place in cake batter.

Devil's Food Cake

½ cup butter at room temperature
1½ cups sugar
2 eggs, separated
1½ cups buttermilk, divided
½ cup cocoa
2 cups sifted cake flour
1½ teaspoons baking soda
1 teaspoon vanilla

Preheat oven to 375°. Cream butter in bowl. Add sugar a little at a time, creaming after each addition until mixture is light and fluffy. Add egg yolks and blend thoroughly.

Add enough buttermilk to cocoa to make smooth paste. Add an additional amount to make 1 cupful of cocoa mixture. Add to creamed mixture.

Sift flour, baking soda and ¼ teaspoon salt in bowl and add alternately with sour milk and vanilla to chocolate mixture. Mix thoroughly.

Stiffly beat egg whites and fold gently into batter. Turn into 2 sprayed, floured 9-inch layer cake pans.

Bake for 30 to 40 minutes or until toothpick inserted in center comes out clean. Frost with Caramel Frosting (page 97) or any desired frosting. Serves 18.

If the top of a cake with butter and sugar creamed together cracks when baked, the oven temperature was too high; or the cake was not placed on the center rack.

Foundation Cake

½ cup butter at room temperature
½ teaspoon vanilla
1½ cups sugar
2 eggs, separated
3 cups sifted flour
4 teaspoons baking powder
1 cup milk

Preheat oven to 350°. Cream butter, vanilla and sugar in bowl until light and fluffy. Continue creaming while adding yolks slowly. In separate bowl, sift flour, baking powder and ½ teaspoon salt and add alternately with milk to creamed mixture.

Beat egg whites until stiff. Fold in beaten egg whites. Turn into 2 lightly sprayed 9-inch cake pans. Bake for 25 minutes or until toothpick inserted in center comes out clean. Serves 18.

Yellow Cake

½ cup butter at room temperature
½ teaspoon vanilla
1½ cups sugar
5 eggs, separated
3 cups sifted flour
4 teaspoons baking powder
1 cup milk

Preheat oven to 350°. Cream butter, vanilla and sugar in bowl until light and fluffy. Continue creaming while slowly adding egg yolks only. In separate bowl, sift flour, baking powder and ½ teaspoon salt and add alternately with milk to creamed mixture.

Turn into 2 lightly sprayed 9-inch cake pans. Bake for 25 minutes or until toothpick inserted in center comes out clean. Serves 18.

Chocolate Cake

⅜ cup butter at room temperature
½ teaspoon vanilla
1½ cups sugar
2 eggs, separated
2⅞ cups sifted flour
4 teaspoons baking powder
1 cup milk
2 ounces dark chocolate, melted

Preheat oven to 350°. Cream butter, vanilla and sugar in bowl until light and fluffy. Continue creaming while adding yolks slowly. In separate bowl, sift flour, baking powder and ½ teaspoon salt and add alternately with milk to creamed mixture. Stir in chocolate.

Beat egg whites until stiff. Fold in beaten egg whites. Turn into 2 lightly sprayed 9-inch cake pans. Bake for 25 minutes or until toothpick inserted in center comes out clean. Serves 18.

White Cake

½ cup butter at room temperature
½ teaspoon vanilla
1½ cups sugar
5 eggs, separated
3 cups sifted flour
4 teaspoons baking powder
1 cup milk

Preheat oven to 350°. Cream butter, vanilla and sugar in bowl until light and fluffy. Continue creaming while slowly adding egg whites only. In separate bowl, sift flour, baking powder and ½ teaspoon salt and add alternately with milk to creamed mixture.

Turn into 2 lightly sprayed 9-inch cake pans. Bake for 25 minutes or until toothpick inserted in center comes out clean. Serves 18.

Four-Egg Cake

4 eggs, separated
¾ cup butter at room temperature
1½ cups sugar
3 cups flour
3 teaspoons baking powder
¾ cup milk
2 teaspoons vanilla

Preheat oven to 400°. Separate eggs. Cream yolks, butter and sugar in bowl. In separate bowl, mix and sift flour, baking powder and 1 teaspoon salt.

Add mixture alternately with milk to egg mixture. Beat egg whites stiff. Add vanilla. Fold gently into dough.

Turn into sprayed cupcake cups or into 3 sprayed layer cake pans. Bake cupcakes for 20 minutes; layer cakes for 25 minutes.

Spread layers and top of cake with Seven-Minute Frosting (page 95), to which has been added ½ cup chopped nuts, ¼ cup chopped candied cherries and ½ cup chopped raisins, if desired. Serves 18 to 20.

What makes a cake dense or heavy in texture? If egg yolks and whites are beaten separately for the recipe, the eggs may have been too small, the eggs were not beaten long enough or the flour was not folded in gently. Other reasons could be that the melted butter was too hot when added or the cake was baked at too low a temperature.

Fruit Cake

2 cups butter at room temperature
2 cups packed light brown sugar
7 eggs, separated
2 tablespoon milk
2 tablespoons apple juice
1 pound walnuts, chopped
2 pounds currants
2 pounds raisins, finely chopped
½ pound date meats, finely chopped
½ pound citron, thinly sliced and cut into short strips
4 cups flour
2 teaspoons mace
2 teaspoons ground cinnamon
2 teaspoons baking powder

Preheat oven to 350°. Cream butter in bowl. Gradually add brown sugar and beat for 5 minutes. Beat egg yolks until light and lemon-colored and whites until stiff and dry. Add these to butter-brown sugar mixture, folding egg whites in gently.

Add milk, juice, chopped nuts and fruits, which have been rolled in flour. Lastly, add well-sifted dry ingredients and a little salt.

Beat mixture thoroughly and place in tube pan lined with parchment paper. Bake for 80 to 90 minutes or until toothpick inserted in center comes out clean. Serves 18.

The first fruitcakes were baked by the Romans.

Fudge Cake

½ cup butter at room temperature.
1¼ cups packed brown sugar
1 teaspoon vanilla
2 eggs
3 ounces melted dark chocolate, cooled
2 cups sifted flour
1½ teaspoons baking powder
½ teaspoon baking soda
1 cup milk

Preheat oven to 350°. Cream butter and brown sugar in bowl. Add vanilla. Add eggs, one at a time, beating thoroughly after each addition.

Beat in chocolate gradually. Sift flour, baking powder and baking soda until smooth. Fold dry ingredients alternately with milk into chocolate mixture.

Turn into 2 sprayed 9-inch cake pans. Bake for 25 minutes or until toothpick inserted in center comes out clean. Serves 18.

Use an oven thermometer to make sure your oven's temperature is accurate. Some ovens can vary 25°, 50° or even 75° from the figure shown on the dial.

Gingerbread Loaf

2 cups sifted cake flour
2 teaspoons baking powder
¼ teaspoon baking soda
2 teaspoons ground ginger
1 teaspoon ground cinnamon
⅓ cup butter at room temperature
½ cup sugar
1 egg, well beaten
⅔ cup molasses
¾ cup sour milk or buttermilk
Whipped cream

Preheat oven to 350°. Sift flour, baking powder, baking soda, spices, and ½ teaspoon salt in bowl. In separate bowl, cream butter thoroughly, add sugar gradually and cream until light and fluffy.

Add egg and molasses; then flour misture, alternately with milk. Beat after each addition until smooth. Pour into sprayed loaf pan. Bake for 75 minutes or until toothpick inserted in center comes out clean. Serve with whipped cream. Serves 10 to 12.

Molasses played a big role in trade in the American colonies and continued to be a primary sweetener until after World War I. Molasses was less expensive and more readily available than sugar and was often used to sweeten baked goods like pies, cakes, gingerbread, toffee candy, and cookies.

Gingerbread Shortcake

2 cups flour
1 teaspoon baking powder
1 teaspoon baking soda
1 teaspoon ground ginger
2 teaspoons ground cinnamon
1 cup molasses
⅓ cup butter at room temperature
½ cup buttermilk
1 egg
1 cup whipping cream, whipped

Preheat oven to 375°. Sift dry ingredients in bowl Heat molasses and butter almost to boiling. Add buttermilk and egg to dry ingredients and stir quickly into hot molasses mixture.

Bake in 2 sprayed 8-inch cake pans for 20 to 25 minutes. Cool and cover with whipped cream to serve. Serves 18.

Peach Cake

½ cup butter at room temperature
1 cup sugar
2 eggs
2 cups flour
2 teaspoons baking powder
½ cup milk
1 cup diced fresh peaches

Preheat oven to 375°. Cream butter and sugar in bowl Add eggs, one at a time, beating well. In separate bowl, sift flour with baking powder and ¼ teaspoon salt. Add alternately with milk to first mixture. Add peaches and mix.

Bake in sprayed 9-inch square pan for 30 to 35 minutes. Serve warm with Lemon Sauce (page 91) or top with sweetened whipped cream. Serves 9.

Gumdrop Cake

½ cup butter at room temperature
1 cup sugar
2 eggs, beaten
2¼ cups flour
2 teaspoons baking powder
1 pound gumdrops, black ones removed, chopped fine
¾ cup raisins
1 teaspoon vanilla
¾ cup milk

Preheat oven to 300°. Cream butter, while adding sugar and beaten eggs in bowl. In separate bowl, sift flour, ¼ teaspoon salt and baking powder over chopped candy and raisins. Dredge well.

Add vanilla to milk. Then add flour mixture and milk alternately to first mixture. Stir well to combine. Bake in large sprayed loaf pan for 90 minutes or until toothpick inserted in center comes out clean. Serves 10 to 12.

Honey Cake

1 cup honey
1 cup sugar
½ cup butter, melted and cooled
2 eggs, slightly beaten
2 cups flour
1 teaspoon baking powder
1 teaspoon caraway seeds

Preheat oven to 375°. Cream honey, sugar, butter and eggs in bowl. In seprate bowl, mix and sift flour, baking powder and seeds. Combine mixtures and mix until smooth.

Turn into sprayed tube pan and bake for 30 to 40 minutes or until toothpick inserted in center comes out clean. Serves 18.

Jelly Roll

Cake:

2 eggs
⅞ cup sugar
Grated peel of 1 lemon
1 cup flour
1½ teaspoons baking powder
3 tablespoons milk

Filling:

Jelly
Powdered sugar

Preheat oven to 350°. Beat eggs in bowl. Add sugar and beat well. Add lemon peel. In separate bowl, sift flour with baking powder and ¼ teaspoon salt and add alternately with milk to first mixture.

Pour into 10 x 15-inch pan, lined with waxed paper or parchment paper. Bake for 15 to 20 minutes. Turn out on damp cloth.

Spread with jelly and roll. Wrap in wax paper and cool. Sprinkle with powdered sugar just before serving. Serves 8 to 12.

While there are many variations on cake throughout the world, the cake we know in the U.S. is primarily of British origin.

Layer Cake

⅓ cup butter at room temperature
¾ cup sugar
2 eggs
1½ cups flour
3 teaspoons baking powder
½ cup milk
1 teaspoon vanilla

Preheat oven to 400°. Cream butter, sugar and eggs in bowl. In separate bowl, mix and sift flour, baking powder and ½ teaspoon salt and add alternately with milk to first mixture. Add vanilla and beat thoroughly.

Bake in 2 sprayed 9-inch cake pans for 20 to 25 minutes. Cool. Put layers together with any cream filling, Chocolate Cream Filling (page 92) or Coconut Cream Filling (page 92), for example. Ice top with Powdered Sugar Frosting (page 94). Serves 18.

Plain cakes without frosting can be frozen for 4 to 6 months. Cakes with buttercream frosting can be frozen for 2 to 3 months. Cakes with cooked frosting, cream cheese frosting or whipped cream should not be frozen.

Chocolate Roll

Cake:

4 eggs, separated
½ cup sugar
4 tablespoons cocoa
1 cup flour
1 teaspoon baking powder

Filling:

1 cup cream
½ teaspoon vanilla
2 tablespoons powdered sugar

Preheat oven to 400°. Beat egg whites in bowl until stiff. Add sugar gradually, beating constantly. Beat in egg yolks and 4 tablespoons cold water.

In separate bowl, mix and sift cocoa, flour, baking powder and ½ teaspoon salt and fold into first mixture. Line 10 x 15-inch pan with sprayed paper or parchment paper. Pour batter into pan.

Bake for 15 to 20 minutes. Turn out on damp cloth and cool slightly. Beat cream stiff with vanilla and powdered sugar in bowl and spread on cake. Roll like a jelly roll (page 68). Sprinkle with powdered sugar. Serves 8 to 12.

Chocolate is one of the gifts of the New World. It was cultivated by the Aztecs and the Mayans and was introduced to European after the Spaniards discovered this treat.

Jiffy Cake with Self-Frosting

4 tablespoons butter at room temperature
1 cup sugar
1 egg
½ cup milk
1½ cups sift flour
1½ teaspoons baking powder
1 teaspoon vanilla
½ cup grated sweet chocolate
½ cup chopped almonds

Preheat oven to 350°. Combine butter, sugar, egg, milk, ⅓ teaspoon salt, flour, baking powder and vanilla in bowl. Beat until light and smooth.

Pour into sprayed 10-inch deep tube pan. Mix chocolate and almonds in bowl and spread evenly over cake. Bake for 35 to 40 minutes or until toothpick inserted in center comes out clean. Serves 18.

Always use the right size of pan. Cake batter should fill the pan no more than two-thirds full before baking.

Mile-a-Minute Cake

1¾ cups flour
2 teaspoons baking powder
½ teaspoon ground cinnamon
½ teaspoon ground nutmeg
⅓ cup butter at room temperature
1⅓ cups packed brown sugar
2 eggs
½ cup milk
½ pound dates, pitted and chopped
½ cup nuts, chopped

Preheat oven to 350°. Sift flour. Measure and sift again with baking powder, 1 teaspoon salt and spices in bowl. Combine all ingredients in order given, adding pitted, chopped dates and chopped nuts last. Beat all just until blended.

Bake in sprayed 9-inch square pan for 50 to 60 minutes. Ice with Peanut Butter Frosting (page 98). Serves 9.

If you don't have brown sugar, add molasses to granulated (white) sugar and mix well. The more molasses you add, the darker the sugar becomes.

Chocolate Chip Layer Cake

2¼ cups sifted cake flour
2¼ teaspoons baking powder
½ cup butter at room temperature
1 cup sugar
3 egg whites
¾ cup milk
1½ teaspoons vanilla
1 (8 ounce) package semi-sweet chocolate chips

Preheat oven to 375°. Sift flour, baking powder and ½ teaspoon salt in bowl. In separate bowl, cream butter thoroughly, add sugar gradually and cream until light and fluffy.

Add egg whites, one at a time, beating thoroughly after each. Add flour mixture, alternately with milk, a small amount at a time, beating after each addition until smooth. Add vanilla.

Spray 2 (8 inch) pans, lined with wax paper and spray again. Pour about one-eighth of batter into each pan. Sprinkle one-eighth of chocolate chips over each lot. Repeat, ending with chocolate.

Bake for 30 minutes or until toothpick inserted in center comes out clean. Frost with your favorite frosting, decorate with shredded chocolate.

To make cupcakes, add chocolate chips to cake batter with vanilla. Bake in sprayed cupcake cups for 20 minutes or until done. Serves 16 to 18.

The ancient Greeks made plakous (the word means flat), a cake made of nuts and honey.

Marble Cake

¾ cup butter at room temperature
2 cups sugar
1½ cups milk
4 egg whites
3¼ cups flour
3 teaspoons baking powder
3 teaspoons vanilla
2 ounces dark chocolate
¼ teaspoon baking soda

Preheat oven to 350°. Cream butter, sugar and 2 tablespoons milk in bowl until light and fluffy. Beat egg whites one at a time into mixture. In separate bowl, sift flour with ½ teaspoon salt and baking powder.

Add sifted dry ingredients alternately with remaining liquid to cream mixture. Add vanilla. Melt chocolate slowly over double boiler and combine with baking soda.

Divide batter into 2 equal parts. Add chocolate mixture to one part. Drop spoonfuls of batter into sprayed, floured 10-inch cake pan, alternating white and chocolate batter until all is used. Bake for 50 minutes or until toothpick inserted in center comes out clean. Serves 20.

At one time, bread and cake were interchangeable words with cake implying a small bread. Primitive man made simple "cakes" with flour from pounded grains and water.

Molasses Cake

½ cup butter at room temperature
½ cup sugar
3 eggs, separated
¾ teaspoon baking soda
⅔ cup molasses
2¼ cups flour
1 teaspoon ground cinnamon
¼ teaspoon ground clove
¼ teaspoon mace
½ cup milk
½ cup raisins

Preheat oven to 350°. Cream butter, sugar and egg yolks in bowl. Add baking soda, mixed with molasses. In seprate bowl, mix and sift flour, cinnamon, clove, mace, and 1 teaspoon salt and add alternately with milk to first mixture.

Beat egg whites and fold into batter. Stir in raisins. Pour into sprayed loaf pan and bake for 50 to 60 minutes or until toothpick inserted in center comes out clean. Serves 10 to 12.

Eggs should be brought close to room temperature (68° to 70°°) by setting them out for 20 to 30 minutes. However, if the recipe calls for separating the eggs, do this when you take them out of the refrigerator because eggs separate more easily when chilled. Just place the separated eggs in bowls, cover and let stand for 20 to 30 minutes to come to room temperature. A large quantity of whites such as a dozen may take 60 minutes to reach room temperature.

Mother's Teacakes

⅓ cup butter at room temperature
1 cup sugar
2 eggs
1½ cups flour
1 teaspoon baking powder
½ cup milk
½ teaspoon vanilla
Powdered sugar

Preheat oven to 400°. Cream butter, sugar, ½ teaspoon salt and eggs in bowl Beat until light and soft. In separate bowl, mix and sift flour and baking powder and add to first mixture alternately with milk. Add vanilla.

Beat thoroughly and pour into sprayed 9 x 13-inch baking pan. Bake for 30 minutes or until toothpick inserted in center comes out clean.

When partly cool, dust with powdered sugar, cut in squares and serve while warm. Serves 20.

At one time, yeast was used to make cakes rise, but by the mid-1700's, beaten eggs became popular as a way to raise cakes by beating in air.

Nun's Cake

1 cup butter at room temperature
1½ cups sugar
5 eggs, separated
3 cups sifted cake flour
2½ teaspoons baking powder
¼ teaspoon mace
¾ cup milk
1 teaspoon vanilla

Preheat oven to 350°. Cream butter in bowl, add sugar gradually and continue creaming. Add egg yolks and 2 egg whites gradually, beating constantly until light and fluffy.

In separate bowl, sift flour, baking powder, 1 teaspoon salt and mace. Add to egg mixture, alternately with milk. Add vanilla. Bake in sprayed 10-inch cake pan for 1 hour or until toothpick inserted in center comes out clean. Serves 18

Quick Orange Cake

½ cup melted butter
1 cup sugar, plus 3 tablespoons
2 eggs, well beaten
¾ cup orange juice
2 cups flour
4 teaspoons baking powder
Peel of 2 oranges

Preheat oven to 350°. Add hot butter to 1 cup sugar in bowl. Add eggs and orange juice. Add sifted dry ingredients and ¼ teaspoon salt and beat well. Pour into sprayed tube pan.

Grate orange peel and mix with 3 tablespoons sugar. Sprinkle on cake. Bake for 50 minutes or until toothpick inserted in center comes out clean. Serves 18.

Peppermint Candy Layer Cake

2⅔ cups flour
3 teaspoons baking powder
½ cup butter at room temperature
1½ cups sugar, divided
1¼ cups milk, divided
1 egg yolk
3 egg whites
1 teaspoon vanilla
½ cup finely ground peppermint stick candy
½ cup coarsely ground peppermint stick candy

Preheat oven to 375°. Sift flour with baking powder and 1 teaspoon saltin bowl. In separate bowl, ream butter. Continue creaming, gradually adding ¾ cup sugar and 3 tablespoons milk.

Add 1 egg yolk and vanilla to remaining milk. Add sifted dry ingredients alternately with milk to creamed mixture.

Beat egg whites stiff but not dry. Beat in remaining sugar. Fold into cake batter.

Pour into 2 sprayed 9-inch layer pans with wax paper or parchment paper in bottom. Sprinkle with finely ground peppermint candy.

Bake for 25 minutes or until toothpick inserted in center comes out clean. Ice with Seven-Minute Frosting (page 95), colored pink. Sprinkle coarsely ground peppermint candy over top and sides of cake. Serves 18.

Pound Cake

1 cup butter at room temperature
1½ cups sugar
5 eggs
2 cups flour
⅛ teaspoon mace (optional)
1 teaspoon vanilla

Preheat oven to 350°.

Cream butter and sugar in bowl. Add eggs, one at a time, beating well after the addition of each egg.

Add flour, 1½ teaspoon salt and mace. Add vanilla and beat thoroughly.

Bake in sprayed loaf pan for 60 to 80 minutes or until toothpick inserted in center comes out clean. Serves 10 to 12.

Cakes should be cooled in pans for about 10 to 15 minutes before turning out on a wire rack to cool. Put a couple of paper towels on the rack to keep the wires from leaving an imprint on the cake or breaking the top of the cake.

Fruit Pound Cake

1 cup butter at room temperature
1½ cups sugar
5 eggs
2 cups flour
1 teaspoon vanilla
½ cup seedless raisins
⅓ cup chopped preserved cherries
¼ cup grated orange peel
¼ cup grated lemon peel
¼ cup chopped nuts
⅓ cup almond halves

Preheat oven to 350°. Cream butter and sugar in bowl. Add eggs, one at a time, beating well after addition of each egg. Add flour and 1½ teaspoon salt. Add vanilla and beat thoroughly. Stir in raisins, cherries, orange peel, lemon peel and chopped nuts.

Bake in sprayed loaf pan for 60 to 80 minutes or until toothpick inserted in center comes out clean. Place almond halves on top of cake while still hot. Serves 10 to 12.

If fruit or nuts sink to the bottom of a cake, the pieces may have been too large; or the fruit or nuts were not dusted with flour before being added; or the batter was too wet; or it was baked at too low a temperature.

Lemon Pound Cake

1 cup butter at room temperature
1½ cups sugar
5 eggs
2 cups flour
1 teaspoon vanilla
¼ cup grated lemon peel

Preheat oven to 350°. Cream butter and sugar in bowl. Add eggs, one at a time, beating well after the addition of each egg. Add flour and 1½ teaspoon salt. Add vanilla and lemon peel and beat thoroughly.

Bake in sprayed tube pan for 60 to 80 minutes or until toothpick inserted in center comes out clean. Serves 18.

Quick Cake

1 cup sugar
1½ cups flour
2 teaspoons baking powder
¼ cup melted butter, cooled
2 eggs
Milk (not skim)
1 teaspoon vanilla

Preheat oven to 400°. Mix and sift sugar, flour, baking powder and ½ teaspoon salt in bowl. Put butter in measuring cup, add eggs and fill cup with milk to 1 cup mark. Add liquid to sifted flour mixture. Add vanilla and beat thoroughly.

Bake in 2 sprayed 8-inch layer cake pans for 15 to 20 minutes or until toothpick inserted in center comes out clean. Cool. Spread Fruit Filling (page 93) between 2 layers and ice top with Quick Frosting (page 94). This cake may also be baked in sprayed muffin cups. Serves 18.

Carrot Cake

2 cups flour, sifted
2 cups sugar
1 teaspoon baking powder
1 teaspoon baking soda
1 teaspoon ground cinnamon
4 eggs
1½ cups canola oil
2 cups grated carrots

Preheat oven to 350°. Spray and flour 3 layer cake pans. Sift ¼ teaspoon salt and dry ingredients in bowl. Blend eggs and oil.

Add dry ingredients and mix thoroughly. Stir in carrots. Pour into pans and bake for 30 to 40 minutes.

Frosting:

1 (8 ounce) package cream cheese, softened
½ cup (1 stick) butter
1 teaspoon vanilla
1 (16 ounce) package powdered sugar
1 cup chopped pecans

Beat cream cheese and butter in bowl. Add vanilla and powdered sugar. Frost cake and sprinkle with pecans. Serves 18 to 20.

Pumpkin Cake

½ cup butter at room temperature
1 cup packed brown sugar
½ cup sugar
1 egg or 2 egg yolks
¾ cup mashed or canned pumpkin
2 cups flour
¼ teaspoon baking soda
3 teaspoons baking powder
1 teaspoon ground cinnamon
⅔ cup chopped nuts
⅓ cup sour milk or buttermilk

Preheat oven to 350°. Cream butter, brown sugar and sugar in bowl. Add 1 egg or 2 egg yolks and pumpkin. In separate bowl, sift flour, baking soda, baking powder, 1 teaspoon salt and cinnamon.

Add nuts and dry mixture alternately with sour milk to creamed mixture. Mix well. Turn into 2 sprayed 8-inch layer pans with sprayed paper or parchment paper.

Bake for 25 minutes or until toothpick inserted in center comes out clean. Cool. Put together with Spiced Whipped Cream (page 96) between layers. Serves 18.

The word cake is derived from the Old Norse word kaka.

Snow Cake

¼ cup butter at room temperature
1 cup sugar
1 ⅔ cups flour
½ teaspoon baking powder
½ cup milk
1 teaspoon vanilla
¼ teaspoon almond extract
2 egg whites, beaten

Preheat oven to 350°. Cream butter and sugar in bowl In separate bowl, mix and sift flour and baking powder and add alternately with milk
to creamed mixture. Add vanilla and almond extract. Fold in egg whites.

Turn into sprayed 9-inch cake pan. Bake for 30 to 40 minutes or until toothpick inserted in center comes out clean. Serves 9.

Swedish Teacakes

½ cup butter at room temperature
¼ cup packed brown sugar
1 egg, separated
1 cup sifted flour
½ cup chopped walnuts
Raspberry or strawberry jam

Preheat oven to 300°. Cream butter in bowl and blend in brown sugar. Add egg yolk, then flour. Roll dough into small balls 1 inch in diameter. Dip in egg white, then roll in chopped nuts.

Place on sprayed baking sheet and press centers down with finger. Bake for 5 minutes. Remove and press down centers again, being careful not to burn yourself. Bake for additional 15 minutes. Cool slightly. Fill centers with jam. Yields 12 cakes.

Old-Fashioned Spice Cake

2 cups flour
2 teaspoons baking powder
1 teaspoon ground cinnamon
¼ teaspoon ground nutmeg
¼ teaspoon ground cloves
¼ teaspoon ground allspice
½ cup raisins
1 cup sugar
½ cup butter at room temperature
1 cup milk, divided
1 egg
Whipped cream

Preheat oven to 350°. Sift flour. Measure and sift flour with remaining dry ingredients and 1 teaspoon salt in bowl. Add raisins.

In separate bowl, cream sugar and butter with 2 tablespoons milk. Add egg and mix well. Add sifted dry ingredients alternately with remaining milk.

Bake in sprayed loaf pan for 30 to 40 minutes in sprayed loaf pan or until toothpick inserted in center comes out clean. Serve with whipped cream. Serves 10 to 12.

Preheat your oven 15 to 20 minutes prior to baking. It is important that the oven be at the correct temperature before placing the item in it or you may not get the best results.

Plain Sponge Cake

1 cup sifted flour
4 - 5 eggs, separated
1 cup sugar, divided
2 tablespoons lemon juice
1 teaspoon lemon peel, grated
Powdered sugar (optional)

Preheat oven to 350°. Sift flour. Beat egg yolks until thick and lemon-colored. Gradually add half sugar, beating thoroughly and then lemon juice and peel. Beat until thick.

Beat egg whites and ½ teaspoon salt until they start to peak but will still flow. Fold remaining sugar, then yolk mixture. Fold in flour gently.

Pour batter as soon as it is mixed into tube pan. A tube pan is best, because center opening allows mixture to heat evenly.

Powdered sugar sifted over top makes a more desirable crust. The oven should be ready for the cake as soon as it is mixed and in the pan.

The cake should be baked for 50 to 60 minutes. After baking, invert the cake to cool, but remove from pan before it is entirely cold. Serves 18.

You can get more juice out of a lemon or lime by rolling it firmly on a countertop or work surface or by microwaving it for 20 to 40 seconds before cutting it.

Sunshine Cake

1 cup sifted flour
6 egg whites
3 egg yolks
1 – 1¼ cups sugar
¾ teaspoon cream of tartar
1 teaspoon vanilla or almond extract
½ teaspoon salt
Powdered sugar (optional)

Preheat oven to 350°. Sift flour. Beat egg yolks until thick and lemon-colored. Gradually add half sugar, beating thoroughly and then lemon juice and peel. Beat until thick.

Beat egg whites, cream of tartar, ½ teaspoon salt and vanilla until they start to peak but will still flow. Fold in remaining sugar, then yolk mixture. Fold in flour gently.

Pour batter as soon as it is mixed into tube pan. A tube pan is best, because center opening allows mixture to heat evenly.

Powdered sugar sifted over top makes a more desirable crust. The oven should be ready for the cake as soon as it is mixed and in the pan.

The cake should be baked for 50 to 60 minutes. After baking, invert the cake to cool, but remove from pan before it is entirely cold. Serves 18.

Old-Fashioned Wedding Cake

1 cup butter at room temperature
1¾ cups packed brown sugar
6 eggs
½ cup molasses
1 cup white grape juice
2 cups flour, divided
1½ tablespoons ground cinnamon
1 tablespoon mace
½ tablespoon ground ginger
½ tablespoon ground cloves
1 cup raisins
1 cup currants
1 cup lemon and orange peel, chopped
1 cup citron, chopped

Preheat oven to 225°. Cream butter and brown sugar in bowl.
Add eggs, molasses and grape juice and mix well. In separate bowl,
mix and sift flour, cinnamon, mace, ginger and clove.

Add enough sifted flour mixture to fruit to keep it from sticking
together. Add remaining flour and fruit to first mixture and
beat thoroughly.

Line bottom of tube pan with sprayed paper or parchment paper
and spray sides of pan.

Pour mixture into pan and bake for 3 to 4 hours or until
toothpick inserted in center comes out clean. Ice and decorate
with Ornamental Frosting (page 95). Serves 18.

*TIP: A small pan of water in the oven helps to keep the cake from
burning during long cooking.*

Basic Cupcakes

½ cup butter at room temperature
1 cup sugar
3 eggs
1¾ cups flour
2 teaspoons baking powder
½ cup milk
1 teaspoon vanilla

Preheat oven to 375°. Cream butter, sugar and eggs in bowl until light and fluffy. In separate bowl, sift flour, baking powder and ½ teaspoon salt, and add alternately with milk to creamed mixture. Add vanilla. Beat thoroughly.

Turn into sprayed cupcake cups. Bake for 15 to 20 minutes or until toothpick inserted in center comes out clean. Yields 18 cupcakes.

Sour Cream Cupcakes

1 tablespoon butter at room temperature
1 cup sugar
2 eggs
½ teaspoon baking soda
½ cup sour cream
1½ cups flour
½ teaspoon cream of tartar
⅛ teaspoon mace

Preheat oven to 400°. Cream butter, sugar and eggs in bowl until light and fluffy. Dissolve baking soda in sour cream.

In separate bowl, sift flour, 1½ teaspoon salt, cream of tartar and mace and add alternately with cream to first mixture. Beat thoroughly. Bake in sprayed cupcake cups for 15 to 20 minutes. Yields 18 cupcakes.

Frostings

Frosting a cake makes it more beautiful and more delicious. Frosting can be applied in one coat or two. If only using one coat, make sure both the cake and the frosting are at room temperature.

Use the thickest and most even layer for the bottom, if making a layer cake. This will provide a better foundation for the cake.

The frosting should be easy to spread. If it is too thick, dilute with a drop or two of milk. Using a knife or an offset spatula, glide the frosting over the cake's surface. Try not to touch the surface of the cake with the spatula, as that can result in crumbs getting in the frosting. Fill the layers and frost the top of the cake before worrying about the sides.

Applying the frosting in two layers uses a "crumb coat." A crumb coat is a thin layer of frosting that is applied first. It does not need to be neat. It should be applied evenly, and as thinly as possible, using a knife or an offset spatula. The frosting should then be allowed to set, either by resting for 40 minutes at room temperature, or by being refrigerated for 10 minutes. The second coat can then be applied. The advantage of the crumb coat is that it makes it easier to get a smooth, crumb-free surface on the cake. It looks better and is easier to decorate.

Lemon Sauce

1 tablespoon cornstarch
½ cup sugar
1 teaspoon grated lemon peel
2 tablespoons lemon juice
2 tablespoons butter
Ground nutmeg

Combine cornstarch, sugar, lemon peel and lemon juice in saucepan. Bring to a boil over medium heat. Boil for 5 minutes. Remove from heat. Add butter. Season to taste with a little nutmeg and salt. Serves 4.

Cream Filling

⅓ cup flour
1 cup sugar
2 cups milk
2 tablespoons butter
3 egg yolks, beaten
½ tablespoon vanilla

Mix flour, sugar and ¼ teaspoon salt in bowl. Bring milk in saucepan to a boil and remove from heat. Add slowly to dry mixture, stirring while adding.

Cook in double boiler, stirring until thick, about 15 minutes. Add butter. Pour mixture over egg yolks, stirring constantly. Cool. Add vanilla. Yields filling for 2 cake layers.

Chocolate Cream Filling

⅓ cup flour
1 cup sugar
2 cups milk
2 ounces dark chocolate syrup
2 tablespoons butter
3 egg yolks, beaten
½ tablespoon vanilla

Mix flour, sugar and ¼ teaspoon salt in bowl. Bring milk and chocolate in saucepan to a boil and remove from heat. Add slowly to dry mixture, stirring while adding.

Cook in double boiler, stirring until thick, about 15 minutes. Add butter. Pour mixture over egg yolks, stirring constantly. Cool. Add vanilla. Yields filling for 2 cake layers.

Coconut Cream Filling

⅓ cup flour
1 cup sugar
2 cups milk
2 tablespoons butter
3 egg yolks, beaten
½ tablespoon vanilla
1 cup shredded coconut

Mix flour, sugar and ¼ teaspoon salt. Bring milk to a boil in saucepan and remove from heat. Add slowly to dry mixture, stirring while adding.

Cook in double boiler, stirring until thick, about 15 minutes. Add butter. Pour mixture over egg yolks, stirring constantly. Cool. Add vanilla and coconut. Yields filling for 2 cake layers.

Fruit Filling

¾ cup chopped dried figs
½ cup chopped dates
¼ cup chopped raisins
½ cup sugar
3 tablespoons lemon juice

Mix figs, dates and raisins in bowl. Add sugar, ½ cup boiling water and lemon juice and cook in double boiler until thick, about 10 minutes. Spread while hot between layers of cake. Yields filling for 1 cake layer.

Marshmallow Cream Filling

¾ cup sugar
⅓ cup corn syrup
16 large marshmallows, cut in quarters
2 egg whites, stiffly beaten

Cook sugar, corn syrup and ¼ cup water in saucepan until it spins a long thread (240°) when dropped from metal spoon.

Remove from heat and immediately add marshmallows. Beat until thoroughly blended. Pour hot syrup over egg whites and continue beating until mixture is smooth. Yields filling for 1 cake layer.

Sugar was once sold in solid shapes of blocks, loaves and cones.

Pineapple Filling

½ cup sugar
¼ cup flour
1 egg, beaten
1 cup chopped pineapple
¾ cup pineapple juice
1 tablespoon butter

Mix sugar, flour and ⅛ teaspoon salt in bowl. Add egg, pineapple and juice. Cook in double boiler until thick, stirring constantly. Add butter and mix well. Cool. Yields filling for 1 cake layer .

Quick Frosting

1 cup sugar
1 egg white
½ teaspoon vanilla

Combine sugar, ¼ cup water and egg white in saucepan and cook in double boiler. Beat constantly until frosting is proper consistency to spread. Add vanilla. Yields frosting for 1 cake layer.

Powdered Sugar Frosting

1½ tablespoons butter
1½ cups powdered sugar
3 tablespoons cream
1 teaspoon vanilla

Cream butter in bowl and continue creaming while slowly adding powdered sugar. Add cream, ⅛ teaspoon salt and vanilla and mix smooth. Add food coloring as desired. Yields frosting for 1 cake layer.

Seven-Minute Frosting

2¼ cups sugar
3 egg whites
1½ tablespoons white corn syrup
1½ teaspoons vanilla

Combine all ingredients, except vanilla and 7½ tablespoons water in double boiler and mix well. Bring to a boil and cook for 3 minutes.

Remove from heat but leave over hot water and beat with for 7 minutes or until it reaches spreading consistency. Add vanilla and blend well. Add food coloring as desired. Yields frosting for 2 cake layers.

Ornamental Frosting

1 egg white
2¾ cups powdered sugar, divided
½ teaspoon lemon juice

Beat egg with 1 cup powdered sugar in bowl until stiff. Add lemon juice and beat in. Add remaining powdered sugar, a small amount at a time, beating after each addition. Cool. Any desired coloring may be beat into frosting. Yields frosting for 2 cake layers.

Plain cakes or cakes frosted with buttercream frosting can be stored in a cake keeper or put under a bowl. Cakes with cream cheese frosting or whipped cream should be refrigerated. A cake with a fluffy cooked frosting should be eaten the same day.

Boiled Corn Syrup Frosting

2½ cups sugar
½ cup corn syrup
2 egg whites, well beaten
1 teaspoon vanilla

Cook sugar, corn syrup, ¼ teaspoon salt and ½ cup water in saucepan to firm ball stage (240°). Pour over egg whites slowly, beating vigorously. Add vanilla. Continue beating until frosting stands in peaks. Cool and keep in refrigerator. Yields frosting for 2 cake layers.

Chocolate Frosting

2½ cups sugar
½ cup corn syrup
2 egg whites, well beaten
1 teaspoon vanilla
3 ounces dark chocolate, melted

Cook sugar, corn syrup, ¼ teaspoon salt and ½ cup water in saucepan to firm ball stage (240°). Pour over egg whites slowly, beating vigorously. Add vanilla and chocolate. Continue beating until frosting stands in peaks. Cool and keep in refrigerator. Yields frosting for 2 cake layers.

Spiced Whipped Cream

1 cup whipping cream
3 tablespoons powdered sugar
1 teaspoon ground cinnamon
1 teaspoon ground ginger

Whip cream in bowl until stiff and add powdered sugar and spices. Yields frosting for 2 cake layers,

Caramel Frosting

2 cups packed brown sugar
1 cup sugar
1 cup sour cream or milk
1 tablespoon butter
1 teaspoon vanilla
¼ cup cream, or as needed

Combine brown sugar, sugar and sour cream in large saucepan and cook over low heat until sugars are dissolved. Cook until a little mixture dropped in cold water forms a soft ball (about 238°).

Remove from heat, add butter and vanilla and cool to 145° or until outside of saucepan feels warm (but not hot) to the touch. Beat until quite stiff, then add enough cream while beating to make of spreading consistency. Yields frosting and fills 2-layer cake, 8-inches in diameter.

Orange Frosting

1 teaspoon light corn syrup
⅞ cup sugar
¼ teaspoon grated orange peel
1 egg white
3 tablespoons orange juice
½ teaspoon lemon juice

Beat all ingredients and a little salt except lemon juice in double boiler. Boil and beat constantly for 6 to 7 minutes, until stiff enough to stand in peaks.

Remove from heat. Add lemon juice. Continue beating until right consistency to spread. Yields frosting for 2 cake layers.

Peanut Butter Frosting

2 cups powdered sugar
3 tablespoons peanut butter
1 teaspoon ground cinnamon
1 teaspoon ground nutmeg
2 - 4 tablespoons milk

Combine powdered sugar, peanut butter, cinnamon and nutmeg in bowl. Add milk slowly while beating until right consistency is reached. Yields frosting for 2 cake layers.

Meringue

3 egg whites
¼ teaspoon vanilla
1 teaspoon lemon juice
6 tablespoons sugar

Beat egg whites in bowl until foamy. Add ¼ teaspoon salt, vanilla and lemon juice. Continue beating until egg whites form thick foam.

Add sugar, 1 tablespoon at a time, beating after each addition. After last addition of sugar, beat until mixture forms soft peaks and sugar is dissolved. Yields for 1 pie.

Lemon Meringue

2 egg whites
4 tablespoons sugar
1 teaspoon lemon juice

Beat egg whites in bowl until frothy. Continue beating while adding sugar gradually until egg holds its shape in soft peaks. Fold in lemon juice. Yields for 1 pie.

Cookies,
Bars
&
Brownies

Yummy treats with
old-fashioned goodness!

Cookies, Bars & Brownies Contents

Cookies

Many of the rules for cake-making apply to cookie-making as well. Most cookies use a creaming method, for instance. Having the oven preheated, and all of the ingredients measured and at room temperature, will make for excellent cookies.

Using a silicone mat (or silpat) in cookie-making can also make a big difference. Silicone mats can be put directly in top of a normal cookie sheet. They prevent the cookies from sticking and help them to cook more evenly.

Use the middle oven racks when baking cookies. The upper and lower racks may produce burnt or undercooked cookies. If forced to use these racks, be careful to rotate the cookies during baking.

Hermits

1 cup butter at room temperature
1½ cups sugar
3 eggs
3 cups flour
½ teaspoon baking soda
1 teaspoon ground allspice
1 teaspoon ground cinnamon
1 teaspoon ground cloves
1 teaspoon ground nutmeg
1½ cups raisins
½ cup chopped nuts

Preheat oven to 350°. Cream butter, sugar and eggs in bowl until light and fluffy. In separate bowl, sift flour, 1½ teaspoons salt, baking soda, allspice, cinnamon, clove and nutmeg and add to creamed mixture. Add raisins and nuts and mix well. Drop teaspoonfuls of dough onto sprayed cookie sheet. Bake for 15 to 20 minutes. Yields 70 cookies.

Brown Sugar Cookies

7 cups sifted flour
1 tablespoon baking soda
1 tablespoon cream of tartar
4 cups packed brown sugar
1 cup melted butter
4 eggs

Mix ingredients well in bowl and form into logs that are 1½ inches thick. Wrap in plastic wrap and let stand in refrigerator for at least 1 hour. When ready to bake, preheat oven to 400°. Slice and bake for 8 to 10 minutes or until light brown. Yields 100 cookies.

Brown Sugar Wafers

1 cup (2 sticks) butter, softened
¾ cup packed dark brown sugar
1 egg yolk
1 tablespoon vanilla
1¼ cups flour

Beat butter in bowl and gradually add brown sugar. Add egg yolk and vanilla and beat well. Add flour and dash salt and mix well.

Shape dough into 1-inch balls and refrigerate for 2 hours. When ready to bake, preheat oven to 350°. Place on cookie sheet and flatten each cookie. Bake for 10 to 12 minutes. Yields 24 cookies.

Butterscotch Cookies

¾ cup butter at room temperature
¾ cup packed brown sugar
1 teaspoon vanilla
4 cups sifted flour
1 teaspoon baking powder
¼ teaspoon baking soda
2 eggs, well beaten

Cream butter and brown sugar in bowl Add vanilla. In separate bowl, ift flour, baking powder, baking soda and ½ teaspoon salt and add alternately with eggs to creamed mixture, beating well after each addition.

Shape into rolls 3 inches thick and 6 inches long. Wrap each in wax paper or plastic wrap and refrigerate for several hours or overnight. When ready to bake, preheat oven to 375°. Cut in slices and bake for 8 minutes. Yields 36 cookies.

Coconut-Orange Jumbles

¾ cup butter at room temperature
1¼ cups sugar
2 eggs
1 cup shredded coconut
2½ cups sifted flour
½ teaspoon baking soda
¾ cup orange juice
3 tablespoons grated orange peel

Preheat oven to 325°. Cream butter and sugar in bowl. Beat in eggs. Beat in coconut. In separate bowl, sift flour, ¼ teaspoon salt and baking soda and add alternately with orange juice to creamed mixture. Beat until smooth.

Drop teaspoonfuls of mixture onto cookie sheet. Sprinkle with additional coconut and orange peel. Bake for 10 to 12 minutes. Yields 48 cookies.

A 16th century British cookie recipe:

To make Fine Cakes. – *Take fine flowre and good Damaske water you must have no other liqeur but that, then take sweet butter, two or three yolkes of eggs and a good quantity of Suger, and a few cloves, and mace, as your Cookes mouth shall serve him, and a lyttle saffron, and a little Gods good about a spoonful if you put in too much they shall arise, cutte them in squares lyke unto trenchers, and pricke them well, and let your oven be well swept and lay them uppon papers.*

Classic Fruit Cookies

1 (16 ounce) package red candied cherries, chopped
1 (16 ounce) package green candied pineapple, chopped
1 pound chopped pecans
3 cups flour, divided
1 teaspoon baking soda
1 teaspoon ground cinnamon
1 teaspoon ground nutmeg
½ teaspoon ground cloves
½ cup (1 stick) butter, softened
1 cup firmly packed brown sugar
4 eggs
⅓ cup bourbon
¼ cup milk

Preheat oven to 300°. Combine cherries, pineapple, pecans and ½ cup flour in large bowl. Toss to coat fruit and set aside.

In separate bowl, combine remaining flour, baking soda, cinnamon, nutmeg and cloves and set aside. Beat butter and brown sugar in bowl until fluffy. Add eggs and beat well.

Stir in dry ingredients, bourbon and milk and mix well. Stir in fruit mixture. Drop teaspoonfuls of dough onto sprayed cookie sheet and bake for about 20 minutes. Cool. Yields 5 to 6 dozen cookies.

Granulated sugar tends to make cookies crispy. Brown sugar tends to make cookies soft and chewy. The moisture in brown sugar creates the chewy quality.

Lemon Cookies

½ cup (1 stick) butter, softened
1 cup sugar
2 tablespoons lemon juice
2 cups flour

Preheat oven to 350°. Cream butter, sugar and lemon juice in bowl and slowly stir in flour. Drop teaspoonfuls of dough onto cookie sheet. Bake for 14 to 15 minutes. Yields 3 dozen cookies.

Lemonade Treats

1 cup shortening
1¼ cups sugar
2 eggs, well beaten
3 cups flour
1 teaspoon baking soda
1 (6 ounce) can lemonade concentrate, thawed, divided
½ teaspoon lemon extract
Extra sugar

Preheat oven to 350°. Cream shortening and sugar in mixing bowl and beat in eggs. In separate bowl, combine flour, baking soda and ½ teaspoon salt. Add alternately with half lemonade concentrate and lemon extract to shortening mixture and mix well.

Drop teaspoonfuls of dough onto sprayed cookie sheet and bake for 12 to 15 minutes. (Cookies do not need to brown.) Before removing from cookie sheet, brush tops of cookies with remaining lemonade concentrate. Sprinkle with sugar and remove from cookie sheet to cool. Yields 3 to 4 dozen cookies.

Banana-Oatmeal Cookies

1 cup (2 sticks) butter, softened
1 cup sugar
1 cup packed brown sugar
2 eggs
1 cup (2 - 3 whole) mashed bananas
2 teaspoons vanilla
2 cups quick-cooking oats
2 cups flour
1 teaspoon baking powder
1 cup chopped pecans
Powdered sugar

Preheat oven to 350°. Cream butter, sugar, brown sugar and eggs in bowl and beat well. Add bananas, vanilla, oats, flour and baking powder and mix well. Stir in pecans.

Drop teaspoonfuls of dough onto sprayed cookie sheet and bake for 12 to 14 minutes. Sift powdered sugar over warm cookies. Cool. Yields 4 dozen cookies.

TIP: Place cookies about 1 inch apart to allow them to spread when baked.

Apple Chip Cookies

1 cup shortening
1½ cups packed brown sugar
⅓ cup light corn syrup
2 eggs
3 cups flour
1 teaspoon baking soda
1 teaspoon ground cinnamon
¼ teaspoon ground cloves
¼ teaspoon ground nutmeg
¾ cup chopped walnuts
1 cup peeled, grated cooking apples
1 (6 ounce) package butterscotch chips

Preheat oven to 350°. Cream shortening, brown sugar, corn syrup and eggs in bowl and beat well. Add flour, ½ teaspoon salt, baking soda, cinnamon, cloves and nutmeg and mix well.

Stir in walnuts, apples and butterscotch chips and mix well. Drop teaspoonfuls of dough onto sprayed cookie sheet and bake for 12 minutes or until cookies brown slightly. Yields 4 dozen cookies.

Cookies and their ingredients spread from Arabian countries to Europe. In the 1300's, little filled wafers were sold by street vendors in Paris, France.

Applesauce Yummies

4 cups flour
2 teaspoons baking soda
1 teaspoon ground cinnamon
1 teaspoon ground nutmeg
½ teaspoon ground allspice
1 cup (2 sticks) butter, softened
1½ cups sugar
1½ cups packed brown sugar
3 eggs, beaten
2 cups applesauce
1 cup golden raisins
1½ cups chopped walnuts

Preheat oven to 400°. Combine flour, baking soda, 1 teaspoon salt, cinnamon, nutmeg and allspice in bowl.

In separate bowl, combine butter and sugar and brown sugar and beat until fluffy. Stir in eggs and applesauce. Add dry ingredients and mix well. Stir in raisins and walnuts.

Drop teaspoonfuls of dough onto sprayed cookie sheet and bake for 8 to 10 minutes or just until cookies brown lightly. Yields 5 to 6 dozen cookies.

What we call cookies in the U.S. are called biscuits in Great Britain and Australia.

Rich Date Cookies

1½ cups sugar, divided
2 cups chopped pitted dates
4 cups flour
1 teaspoon baking soda
1 cup (2 sticks) butter, softened
1 cup packed brown sugar
3 eggs
1 teaspoon vanilla
1½ cups chopped pecans

Preheat oven to 350°. Cook and stir ½ cup sugar, dates and ½ cup water in saucepan over medium heat until mixture thickens. Set aside to cool.

Combine flour, baking soda and 1 teaspoon salt in large bowl and set aside.

In separate bowl, cream butter, 1 cup sugar and brown sugar and mix well. Blend in eggs and vanilla. Add dry ingredients and mix well. Stir in pecans and cooked dates.

Drop teaspoonfuls of dough onto sprayed cookie sheet and bake for 12 to 14 minutes. Cool and store in airtight container. Yields 4 dozen cookies.

The earliest cookies known historically date from the 7th century in Persia (modern day Iran).

Orange-Nut Drops

½ cup (1 stick) butter, softened
1 (3 ounce) package cream cheese, softened
¾ cup sugar
1 egg, beaten
1 teaspoon orange extract
1 tablespoon grated orange peel
1 cup flour
¾ cup chopped walnuts

Preheat oven to 350°. Cream butter, cream cheese and sugar in bowl and beat until creamy. Add egg, orange extract and orange peel and mix well. Fold in flour and ½ teaspoon salt and mix well. Stir in walnuts.

Drop teaspoonfuls of dough onto sprayed cookie sheet and bake for 12 to 15 minutes or until cookies brown slightly. Cool before storing. Yields 3 dozen cookies.

Drop Cookies

¾ cup butter at room temperature
3 teaspoons vanilla
1½ cups sugar
2 eggs, well beaten
4 cups sifted flour
4 teaspoons baking powder
¾ cup milk

Preheat oven to 400°. Cream butter, vanilla and sugar in bowl until light and fluffy. Continue creaming while adding eggs. In separate bowl, sift flour, baking powder and ½ teaspoon salt and add alternately with milk to creamed mixture.

Drop small portions of mixture onto sprayed cookie sheet and bake for 12 to 15 minutes. Yields 72 cookies.

Crisp Cookies

1 cup butter at room temperature
2 teaspoons vanilla
2 cups sugar
2 eggs
4 cups sifted flour
4 teaspoons baking powder
¼ cup milk

Cream butter, vanilla and sugar in bowl until light and fluffy. Continue creaming while adding eggs. In separate bowl, sift flour, baking powder and ½ teaspoon salt and add alternately with milk to creamed mixture.

Form dough into roll 3 inches thick and 6 inches long. Wrap in wax paper or plastic wrap and refrigerate.

When ready to bake, preheat oven to 375°. Cut off thin slices and bake for 10 to 12 minutes. Yields 72 cookies.

Crisp cookies and soft cookies should not be stored together or the moisture in the soft cookies will cause the crisp ones to soften.

Rolled Cookies

1 cup butter at room temperature
2 teaspoons vanilla
2 cups sugar
2 eggs
4 cups sifted flour
4 teaspoons baking powder
¼ cup milk

Preheat oven to 375°. Cream butter, vanilla and sugar in bowl until light and fluffy. Continue creaming while adding eggs. In separate bowl, sift flour, baking powder and ½ teaspoon salt and add alternately with milk to creamed mixture.

Roll on lightly floured board to ¼ inch thickness. Cut into any desire shape and bake on sprayed cooket sheet. for 10 to 12 minutes. Yields 72 cookies.

Gingersnaps

1 cup sugar
1 cup molasses
1 cup butter at room temperature
1 egg
1 teaspoon ground cinnamon
2 teaspoons ground ginger
2 teaspoons baking soda
1 tablespoon cider vinegar
1 teaspoon vanilla
2½ cups flour, more if needed

Preheat oven to 325°. Combine sugar, molasses, butter, egg, cinnamon, ginger and baking soda in bowl. Mix well. Add vinegar, vanilla and enough flour to make stiff dough. Roll very thin. Cut with cookie cutter. Bake for 10 to 12 minutes. Yields 48 gingersnaps.

Ginger Cookies

½ cup butter at room temperature
½ cup molasses
½ cup sugar
½ teaspoon ground nutmeg
½ teaspoon ground cinnamon
½ teaspoon ground ginger
1 egg, beaten
½ cup chopped walnuts
2½ cups flour
½ teaspoon baking powder

Cream butter, molasses, sugar, nutmeg, cinnamon and ginger in medium saucepan. Mix well and bring slowly to boiling point. Cool.

Add egg and nuts, combining well. Sift flour, baking powder and ⅔ teaspoon salt in bowl and add to first mixture. Mix thoroughly.

Shape into roll about 2½ inches thick. Roll in wax paper or plastic wrap and refrigerate for at least 1 hour.

When ready to bake, preheat oven to 375°. Slice and bake for 12 minutes. Yields 48 cookies.

The best way to keep refrigerated cookie dough from getting flat on one side when you are slicing it is to roll it on the countertop after each slice. Another method is to roll it one-fourth of the way around after each slice.

Almond Macaroons

3 egg whites
1 cup sugar
½ pound finely ground almonds
½ teaspoon almond extract
1 tablespoon melted butter

Preheat oven to 275°. Beat egg whites in bowl. Add sugar gradually, beating constantly. Add almonds, flavoring and butter. Mix well.

Drop teaspoonfuls of mixture on sprayed cookie sheet. Bake for 30 to 40 minutes. Yields 48 macaroons.

Coconut Macaroons

2 (7 ounce) packages flaked coconut
1 (14 ounce) can sweetened condensed milk
2 teaspoons vanilla
½ teaspoon almond extract

Preheat oven to 350°. Combine coconut, sweetened condensed milk, vanilla and almond extract in bowl and mix well.

Drop rounded teaspoonfuls of dough onto foil-lined cookie sheet.

Bake for 8 to 10 minutes or until light brown around edges. Immediately remove from foil. (Macaroons will stick if allowed to cool.) Store at room temperature. Yields 3 dozen macaroons.

Cookie recipes expanded in variety with modern transportation. Railroads allowed the shipment of coconuts, oranges and other foods. When cornflakes were invented, this and other cereal products became ingredients.

Chocolate Macaroons

4 (1 ounce) package sweet baking chocolate
2 egg whites, room temperature
½ cup sugar
¼ teaspoon vanilla
1 (7 ounce) can flaked coconut

Preheat oven to 350°. Stir and melt chocolate in double boiler. Remove from heat and cool.

Beat egg whites in small bowl at high speed for 1 minute. Gradually add sugar 1 tablespoon at a time and beat until stiff peaks form (about 3 minutes).

Add ¼ teaspoon salt, chocolate and vanilla and beat well. Stir in coconut.

Drop teaspoonfuls of mixture onto cookie sheet lined with brown paper and bake for 12 to 15 minutes. Transfer cookies to cooling rack. Yields 3 dozen cookies.

Historians believe that macaroons were first made in an Italian monastery in the Middle Ages.

Hazelnut Cookies

4 ounces milk chocolate
¼ pound finely chopped hazelnuts
¼ pound finely chopped almonds
⅔ cup powdered sugar
2 egg whites
¼ teaspoon ground cinnamon
Few grains ground clove
2 tablespoons butter, melted

Melt chocolate in double boiler. Add chopped nuts and powdered sugar and mix well. Add stiffly beaten egg whites, spices and butter. Mix well. Shape into roll about 2½ inches thick. Refrigerate.

When ready to bake, preheat oven to 325°. Roll out thin, a small quantity at a time, on slightly floured board. Cut with cookie cutter. Placed on sprayed cookie sheets and bake for 12 to 15 minutes. Yields 4 dozen cookies.

In western Europe, cookies were first used as a means to test the oven temperature for cakes. If a small amount of batter baked well, then the temperature was right for the cake.

Oatmeal Lace Wafers

2 tablespoons butter at room temperature
1 cup sugar
2 eggs
½ teaspoon ground nutmeg
2½ cups old-fashioned oats
2½ teaspoons baking powder
1 teaspoon vanilla
¼ teaspoon almond extract

Preheat oven to 350°. Cream butter, sugar and eggs in bowl until light and fluffy. In separate bowl, combine ½ teaspoon salt, nutmeg, oats and baking powder and add to creamed mixture. Mix thoroughly. Add vanilla and almond extract.

Drop teaspoonfuls of mixture on sprayed cookie sheet. Bake for 12 to 15 minutes. Yields 60 cookies.

Oatmeal Cookies

1½ cups old-fashioned oats
½ cup packed brown sugar
¾ cup flour
½ teaspoon baking soda
½ teaspoon ground cinnamon
¼ cup milk
½ cup butter, melted

Combine oats, brown sugar, flour, 1 teaspoon salt, baking soda and cinnamon in bowl. Add milk and melted butter. Mix well. Roll into ball and wrap in wax paper or plastic wrap. Refrigerate for at least 1 hour.

When ready to bake, preheat oven to 350°. Roll out ¼ inch thick on slightly floured board. Cut into circles and place on cookie sheet. Bake for 12 to 15 minutes. Yields 60 cookies.

Oatmeal-Raisin Cookies

1½ cups flour
½ teaspoon baking powder
¼ teaspoon ground nutmeg
1 cup (2 sticks) butter, softened
1 cup sugar
1 cup packed brown sugar
2 large eggs
3 cups quick-cooking oats
1½ cups golden raisins

Preheat oven to 325°. Combine flour, baking powder, nutmeg and ½ teaspoon salt in bowl and set aside.

In separate bowl, beat butter, sugar and brown sugar until creamy. Beat in eggs, one at a time. Reduce speed to low and slowly mix in flour mixture. Mix in oats and raisins.

Using ¼ cup measure of dough, roll dough into balls and place on cookie sheet 2½ inches apart. Flatten cookies slightly using your palm and bake for 22 to 25 minutes.

Let cookies cool on cookie sheets for 10 minutes and transfer to wire rack. Cool completely before storing. Yields 2 dozen large cookies.

Cookies are perhaps the easiest thing to bake and are a good place for a novice baker to start.

Old-Fashioned Everyday Oatmeal Cookies

1 cup sugar
1 cup packed brown sugar
1 cup shortening
2 eggs
2 teaspoons vanilla
1 teaspoon baking soda
1½ cups flour
3 cups quick-cooking oats
1 cup chopped pecans

Preheat oven to 350°. Combine sugar, brown sugar, shortening, eggs, 2 tablespoons water and vanilla in bowl and beat well.

Add 1 teaspoon salt, baking soda and flour and mix well. Pour in oats and pecans and mix.

Drop teaspoonfuls of dough onto cookie sheet and bake for 14 to 15 minutes or until cookies brown. Yields 4 to 5 dozen cookies.

The Quaker Company is the largest producer of oats in America. The original package was square. The familiar cylinder shape was introduced in 1915.

Peanutty Oatmeal Cookies

½ cup (1 stick) butter, softened
2 cups sugar
1½ cups packed brown sugar
4 eggs, beaten
1 teaspoon vanilla
1 (16 ounce) jar chunky peanut butter
6 cups quick-cooking oats
2½ teaspoons baking soda
1 (6 ounce) package butterscotch chips

Preheat oven to 350°. Beat butter, sugar, brown sugar, eggs and vanilla in bowl on low speed until smooth. Fold in peanut butter and mix well.

Stir in oats, baking soda and butterscotch chips with wooden spoon and mix well.

Drop tablespoonfuls of dough onto cookie sheet and flatten with fork. Bake for 8 to 10 minutes and cool. Yields 4 dozen cookies.

The first cookbook written by an American and published in the U.S. was American Cookery by Amelia Simmons. It included two recipes for cookies. Here is the one entitled "Christmas Cookey":

To three pound of flour, sprinkle a tea cup of fine powdered coriander seed, rub in one pound of butter, and one and half pound sugar, dissolve one tea spoonful of pearlash in a tea cup of milk, kneed all together well, roll three quarter of an inch thick, and cut or stamp into shape and size you please, bake slowly fifteen or twenty minutes; tho' hard and dry at first, if put in an earthern pot, and dry cellar, or damp room, they will be finer, softer and better when six months old.

Cocoa-Oatmeal Cookies

1 cup (2 sticks) butter, softened
1⅔ cups sugar
2 eggs
2 teaspoons vanilla
¾ teaspoon baking soda
1½ cups flour
3 tablespoons cocoa
1 teaspoon ground cinnamon
2½ cups quick-cooking oats
1 cup chopped pecans

Preheat oven to 350°. Cream butter, sugar, eggs and vanilla in bowl.

In separate bowl, combine baking soda, ½ teaspoon salt, flour, cocoa and cinnamon and gradually add to sugar mixture. Stir in oats and pecans.

Drop teaspoonfuls of dough onto cookie sheet and bake for 15 to 18 minutes. Yields 4 dozen cookies.

The name cookie comes from koekje, a Dutch word meaning a "little cake".

Pecan Wafers

½ cup butter at room temperature
1 cup packed brown sugar
2 eggs
4 tablespoons flour
½ cup chopped pecans
½ teaspoon maple syrup

Preheat oven to 300°. Cream butter and brown sugar in bowl. Add eggs, one at a time, beating well after each is added. Stir in flour and blend well. Add nuts, ½ teaspoon salt and syrup.

Drop teaspoonfuls of mixture, 5 inches apart on sprayed cookie sheet. Spread out very thin with spoon. Bake for 10 to 12 minutes. If desired, these may be turned around finger to form rolls while warm. Yields 36 wafers.

Pecan Puffs

2 egg whites
¾ cup packed light brown sugar
1 teaspoon vanilla
1 cup chopped pecans

Preheat oven to 250°. Beat egg whites in bowl until foamy. Gradually add (¼ cup at a time) brown sugar and vanilla. Continue beating until stiff peaks form (about 3 or 4 minutes). Fold in pecans.

Line cookie sheet with freezer paper. Drop teaspoonfuls of mixture onto paper. Bake for 45 minutes. Yeilds 3 dozen cookies.

Peanut Butter Cookies

2 cups sifted flour
1½ teaspoons baking powder
2 tablespoons butter at room temperature
½ cup peanut butter
1 cup sugar
1 egg
1 teaspoon vanilla
⅓ cup milk
½ cup peanuts, chopped

Sift flour, baking powder and ½ teaspoon salt in bowl. In separate bowl, cream butter and peanut butter. Beat in remaining ingredients (except chopped peanuts) one at a time. Stir in flour mixture, blending well. Roll into ball and cover with wax paper or plastic wrap. Refrigerate for at least 1 hour.

When ready to bake, preheat oven to 350°. Roll out to ¼ inch thickness on slightly floured board. Cut with cookie cutter. Place on cookie sheet. Sprinkle with peanuts. Bake for 12 to 15 minutes. Yields 50 cookies.

To keep cookie dough from sticking and getting tough when rolling it out, sprinkle a mixture of flour and powdered sugar on the work surface.

Cinnamon-Peanut Cookies

½ cup (1 stick) butter, softened
½ cup sugar
½ cup packed brown sugar
½ cup peanut butter
1 egg
1 teaspoon vanilla
1 cup flour
1 teaspoon ground cinnamon
½ cup peanuts

Preheat oven to 350°. Combine butter, sugar, brown sugar, peanut butter, egg and vanilla in bowl and beat well. Add flour, ½ teaspoon salt and cinnamon and mix well. Stir in peanuts.

Drop teaspoonfuls of dough onto cookie sheet and bake for 10 to 12 minutes. Yields 2½ dozen cookies.

Corn Flake Cookies

1 cup butter at room temperature
1½ cups sugar
2 eggs, well beaten
¼ cup milk
1 cup raisins
2 cups flour, plus more for rolling out
2 teaspoons baking soda
2 cups corn flakes

Preheat oven to 350°. Cream butter and sugar. in bowl Add eggs and beat until light. Add milk and raisins. In separate bowl, sift flour with baking soda and add, blending well. Add corn flakes.

Roll ¼ inch thick on slightly floured board. Cut with cookie cutter. Place on cookie sheet and bake for 12 to 15 minutes. Yields 48 cookies.

Old-Fashioned Peanut Butter Cookies

1 cup shortening
1 cup crunchy or creamy peanut butter
1 cup sugar
1 cup packed brown sugar
1 teaspoon vanilla
2 eggs, well beaten
2½ cups flour
1 teaspoon baking soda
1 teaspoon baking powder

Preheat oven to 350°. Cream shortening and peanut butter in bowl. Add sugar, brown sugar and vanilla and mix well. Stir in beaten eggs.

In separate bowl, combine flour, baking soda, baking powder and ½ teaspoon salt. Pour into peanut butter mixture in small batches and mix well after each addition.

Form into 1 to 2-inch balls and arrange on cookie sheet about 2 inches apart. Dip fork into water and flatten slightly with tines of fork. Use criss-cross pattern with fork to flatten a little more. Bake for about 10 to 12 minutes. Yields 3 to 4 dozen cookies.

How do you identify an authentic peanut butter cookie... by the criss-cross design on top, of course! This practice dates back to 1931 in Pillsbury's Balanced Recipes with "Peanut Butter Balls" flattened with a fork before baking.

Peanut Butter-Date Cookies

1 egg, beaten
⅔ cup sugar
⅓ cup packed brown sugar
1 cup chunky peanut butter
½ cup flour
½ cup chopped dates

Preheat oven to 350°. Blend egg, sugar, brown sugar, peanut butter and flour in bowl and mix thoroughly. Stir in dates and roll into 1-inch balls.

Place on unsprayed cookie sheet. Use fork to press ball down to about ½ inch. Bake for about 12 minutes. Cool before storing. Yields 2 dozen cookies.

Molasses Crisps

¼ cup butter
½ cup sugar
¾ cup molasses
1 cup flour

Preheat oven to 350°. Melt butter in saucepan. Add sugar and molasses and bring to boiling point. Cool slightly. Add flour and ¾ teaspoon salt.

Drop teaspoonfuls of mixture onto sprayed cookie sheet. Bake for 12 to 15 minutes. Yields 36 cookies.

A cookie sheet is a rectangular pan about 14 x 16 inches with no sides. A baking sheet is a rectangular pan about 10 x 15 inches with 1-inch sides. A 9 x 13 inch baking pan has sides 2 to 3 inches high.

Sugar Cookies

⅔ cup butter at room temperature
1¼ cups sugar, plus more for sprinkling
2 eggs
3 cups flour
2 teaspoons baking powder
Grated peel of 1 lemon
1 tablespoon freshly squeezed lemon juice

Cream butter, sugar and eggs in bowl until light and foamy. In separate bowl, sift flour, 1½ teaspoon salt and baking powder and add to first mixture. Add lemon peel and juice. Mix until smooth.

Roll into ball and wrap in wax paper or plastic wrap. Refrigerate for at least 1 hour.

When ready to bake, preheat oven to 350°. Roll to ¼ inch thickness on slightly floured board. Cut with cookie cutter. Sprinkle with sugar and bake for 12 to 15 minutes. Yields 60 cookies.

Sugar cookies were once round and plain with an unassuming dusting of granulated sugar on top. Today these delicious cookies are a favorite of both professional and amateur bakers who cut them into various shapes and decorate them with frosting, cookie paints and candy. Sugar cookie bouquets are popular for showers, parties and other special occasions.

Almond Cookies

⅔ cup butter at room temperature
1¼ cups sugar, plus more for sprinkling
2 eggs
1 teaspoon vanilla
3 cups flour
2 teaspoons baking powder
½ cup chopped almonds

Cream butter, sugar, eggs and vanilla in bowl until light and foamy. In separate bowl, sift flour, 1½ teaspoon salt and baking powder and add to first mixture. Mix until smooth.

Roll into ball and wrap in wax paper or plastic wrap. Refrigerate for at least 1 hour.

When ready to bake, preheat oven to 350°. Roll to ¼ inch thickness on slightly floured board. Cut with cookie cutter, brush with egg and dip in chopped almonds. Sprinkle with sugar and bake for 12 to 15 minutes. Yields 60 cookies.

When using cookie cutters, particularly plastic ones, dip the cutter in warm vegetable oil so the edges will cut cleanly.

Chocolate Cookies

⅔ cup butter at room temperature
1¼ cups sugar, plus more for sprinkling
2 eggs
1 teaspoon vanilla
½ cup cocoa
3 tablespoons coffee
3 cups flour
2 teaspoons baking powder

Cream butter, sugar, eggs and vanilla in bowl until light and foamy. Add cocoa and coffee and stir. In separate bowl, sift flour, 1½ teaspoon salt and baking powder and add to first mixture. Mix until smooth.

Roll into ball and wrap in wax paper or plastic wrap. Refrigerate for at least 1 hour.

When ready to bake, preheat oven to 350°. Roll to ¼ inch thickness on slightly floured board. Cut with cookie cutter. Sprinkle with sugar and bake for 12 to 15 minutes. Yields 60 cookies.

When making cutout cookies, chill before cutting out.

Fig Cookies

⅔ cup butter at room temperature
1¼ cups packed brown sugar, plus more for sprinkling
2 eggs
1 teaspoon vanilla
3 cups flour
2 teaspoons baking powder
⅔ cup chopped dried figs

Cream butter, brown sugar, eggs and vanilla in bowl until light and foamy. In separate bowl, sift flour, 1½ teaspoon salt and baking powder and add to first mixture. Mix until smooth.

Add figs and mix well. Roll into ball and wrap in wax paper or plastic wrap. Refrigerate for at least 1 hour.

When ready to bake, preheat oven to 350°. Roll to ¼ inch thickness on slightly floured board. Cut with cookie cutter. Sprinkle with sugar and bake for 12 to 15 minutes. Yields 60 cookies.

Because cookies bake quickly, they must be watched and timed with care. Bake 1 or 2 minutes less if you prefer a softer texture.

Halloween Cookies

⅔ cup butter at room temperature
1¼ cups sugar, plus more for sprinkling
2 eggs
3 cups flour
2 teaspoons baking powder
½ teaspoon ground cinnamonm
Grated peel of 1 lemon

Cream butter, sugar and eggs in bowl until light and foamy. In seprate bowl, sift flour, 1½ teaspoon salt, baking powder and cinnamon and add to first mixture. Add lemon peel and juice. Mix until smooth.

Roll into ball and wrap in wax paper or plastic wrap. Refrigerate for at least 1 hour.

When ready to bake, preheat oven to 350°. Roll to ¼ inch thickness on slightly floured board. Cut with cookie cutter. Sprinkle with sugar and bake for 12 to 15 minutes. Ice cookies with Orange Frosting on (page 97). Yields 60 cookies.

You can prepare buttercream frostings in advance (and color them as well), but be sure to cover the bowl with plastic wrap so the frosting does not form a "crust".

Nut Cookies

⅔ cup butter at room temperature
1¼ cups sugar, plus more for sprinkling
2 eggs
3 cups flour
2 teaspoons baking powder
Grated peel of 1 lemon
1 tablespoon freshly squeezed lemon juice
½ cup chopped nuts

Preheat oven to 350°. Cream butter, sugar and eggs in bowl until light and foamy. In seprate bowl, sift flour, 1½ teaspoon salt and baking powder and add to first mixture. Add lemon peel and juice. Mix until smooth.

Drop dough by tablespoonfuls onto sprayed cookie sheet. Flatten with bottom of glass. Brush surface with egg white and sprinkle with chopped nuts and sugar. Bake for 12 to 15 minutes. Yields 60 cookies.

Bakers in medieval England kept their procedures and recipes secret. Someone wanting to become a baker had to serve as an apprentice for 7 years. There were laws passed both regulating baking and protecting the baker's craft.

Sand Tarts

⅔ cup butter at room temperature
1¼ cups sugar, plus more for sprinkling
2 eggs
1 teaspoon vanilla
3 cups flour
2 teaspoons baking powder
2 egg whites
Ground cinnamon
Whole almonds

Cream butter, sugar, eggs and vanilla in bowl until light and foamy. In separate bowl, sift flour, 1½ teaspoon salt and baking powder and add to first mixture. Mix until smooth.

Roll into ball and wrap in wax paper or plastic wrap. Refrigerate for at least 1 hour.

When ready to bake, preheat oven to 350°. Roll to ¼ inch thickness on slightly floured board. Cut into diamonds or squares, brush with white of egg, sprinkle with sugar and ground cinnamon and place an almond in center of each cookie. Bake for 12 to 15 minutes. Yields 60 cookies.

> *It is best to refrigerate the dough before using a cookie cutter or slicing the dough.*

Spice Cookies

⅔ cup butter at room temperature
1¼ cups sugar, plus more for sprinkling
2 eggs
1 teaspoon vanilla
3 cups flour
2 teaspoons baking powder
⅛ teaspoon clove
¼ teaspoon ground nutmeg
½ teaspoon ground cinnamon

Cream butter, sugar, eggs and vanilla in bowl until light and foamy. In seprate bowl, sift flour, 1½ teaspoon salt, baking powder, clove, nutmeg and cinnamon and add to first mixture. Mix until smooth.

Roll into ball and wrap in wax paper or plastic wrap. Refrigerate for at least 1 hour.

When ready to bake, preheat oven to 350°. Roll to ¼ inch thickness on slightly floured board. Cut with cookie cutter. Sprinkle with sugar and bake for 12 to 15 minutes. Yields 60 cookies.

Many historians believe that sugar from sugarcane originated in southern Asia, possibly in Bengal in India.

Filled Cookies

⅔ cup butter at room temperature
1¼ cups sugar, plus more for sprinkling
2 eggs
3 cups flour
2 teaspoons baking powder
Grated peel of 1 lemon
1 tablespoon freshly squeezed lemon juice
1¼ cup jam

Cream butter, sugar and eggs in bowl until light and foamy. In seprate bowl, sift flour, 1½ teaspoon salt and baking powder and add to first mixture. Add lemon peel and juice. Mix until smooth.

Roll into ball and wrap in wax paper or plastic wrap. Refrigerate for at least 1 hour.

When ready to bake, preheat oven to 350°. Roll to ⅛ inch thickness on slightly floured board. Cut into circles. Put 1 teaspoon jam in center of half of the circles. Place remaining circles on top of jam and press edges together firmly. Bake for 12 to 15 minutes. Yields 30 cookies.

TIP: *For additional fillings, boil 1 cup chopped raisins, figs or dates with 1 cup sugar and ¼ cup water until fruit is tender.*

Humidity can affect flour. If a recipe calls for a variable amount such as 1¼ to 1½ cups, add the smaller amount first, then add more if needed for the right consistency.

Cheesecake Cookies

1 cup (2 sticks) butter, softened
2 (3 ounce) packages cream cheese, softened
2 cups sugar
2 cups flour

Preheat oven to 350°. Cream butter and cream cheese in mixing bowl. Add sugar and beat until light and fluffy. Add flour and beat well.

Drop teaspoonfuls of dough onto cookie sheet and bake for 12 to 15 minutes or until edges are golden. Yields 3 dozen cookies.

TIP: These are even better if you add 1 cup chopped pecans.

Scotch Shortbread

½ cup (1 stick) unsalted butter, softened
⅓ cup sugar
1¼ cups flour
Powdered sugar

Preheat oven to 325°. Cream butter and sugar in bowl until light and fluffy. Add flour and pinch of salt and mix well.

Spread dough in 8-inch square pan. Bake for 20 minutes or until light brown. Cool shortbread in pan, dust with powdered sugar and cut into squares. Yields 16 cookies.

Yummy Cookies

3 egg whites
1¼ cups sugar
2 teaspoons vanilla
3½ cups frosted corn flakes
1 cup chopped pecans

Preheat oven to 250°. Beat egg whites in bowl until stiff. Gradually add sugar and vanilla. Fold in frosted corn flakes and pecans. Drop teaspoonfuls of dough onto cookie sheet lined with wax paper. Bake for 40 minutes. Yields 3 dozen cookies.

Brown-Eyed Susans

1 cup (2 sticks) butter, softened
¼ cup sugar
½ teaspoon almond extract
2 cups flour
1 cup powdered sugar
3 tablespoons cocoa
½ teaspoon vanilla
Whole almonds

Preheat oven to 350°. Beat butter and sugar in bowl until light and fluffy. Stir in almond extract. Gradually add flour and ½ teaspoon salt and mix well after each addition.

Form cookie dough into balls and place onto cookie sheet. With bottom of glass or hand, flatten balls slightly. Bake for 13 to 15 minutes or until light brown. Set aside to cool.

Mix powdered sugar and cocoa in bowl and gradually pour in 1½ tablespoons hot water and vanilla. Mix well and frost cookies. Put whole almond on top of each cookie. Yields 3 dozen cookies.

Classic Snickerdoodles

½ cup (1 stick) butter, softened
½ cup shortening
1½ cups plus 4 tablespoons sugar, divided
2 eggs
2¼ cups flour
2 teaspoons cream of tartar
1 teaspoon baking soda
1 teaspoon ground cinnamon

Preheat oven to 350°.

Mix butter, shortening, 1½ cups sugar and eggs in medium bowl and beat well. Stir in flour, cream of tartar, baking soda and ¼ teaspoon salt.

Shape rounded teaspoonfuls of dough into balls.

In separate bowl, mix 4 tablespoons sugar and cinnamon and roll balls in mixture to cover.

Place balls 2 inches apart onto cookie sheet and use bottom of jar or glass to mash cookies flat.

Bake for 8 to 10 minutes or until edges just begin to brown. Yields 4 dozen cookies.

The origin and name of snickerdoodles are unknown; some credit Dutch settlers and others Germans who came to colonial America. Whatever their origin, snickerdoodles have survived and changed little throughout American's history. The dough is made with butter, flour, shortening, and sometimes spices and/or nuts. It is then rolled in or sprinkled with cinnamon and sugar before baking. The surface of the cookie often cracks as it bakes, giving it a distinctive look.

Macadamia Nut Cookies

½ cup shortening
½ cup (1 stick) butter, softened
2½ cups flour, divided
½ cup sugar
1 cup packed brown sugar
2 eggs
1 teaspoon vanilla
½ teaspoon butter flavoring
1 teaspoon baking soda
2 cups white chocolate chips
½ cup chopped macadamia nuts

Preheat oven to 350°. Beat shortening and butter in bowl. Add half flour and mix well. Add sugar, brown sugar, eggs, vanilla, butter flavoring and baking soda and beat until ingredients mix well.

Add remaining flour. Mix well and stir in chocolate chips and nuts. Drop teaspoonfuls of dough onto cookie sheet and bake for about 8 minutes. Yields 4 dozen cookies.

Do not eat raw dough or batter, especially if it contains eggs.
Cover and refrigerate if you are not going to bake it right away.

Chocolate-Nut Cookies

½ cup butter at room temperature
1 cup packed brown sugar
1 egg
2 ounces dark chocolate, melted
1½ cups flour
½ teaspoon baking soda
1 teaspoon baking powder
½ cup milk
1 teaspoon vanilla
1 cup chopped walnuts

Preheat oven to 400°. Cream butter, brown sugar and egg in bowl. Add melted chocolate. In separate bowl, sift flour, ¼ teaspoon salt, baking soda and baking powder.

Add sifted dry ingredients alternately with milk and vanilla, and add nuts last. Drop on cookie sheet. Bake for 15 to 20 minutes. Yields 24 cookies.

Help! I forgot to take the butter out of the refrigerator! Do not melt the butter, but just cut into small pieces and place on a plate and it will warm up quickly.

Chocolate-Walnut Cookies

½ cup butter at room temperature
1 cup sugar
1 egg
1 teaspoon vanilla
2½ cups flour
1 teaspoon baking powder
½ teaspoon ground cinnamon
2 tablespoons milk
2 ounces melted dark chocolate
½ cup chopped walnuts

Cream butter, sugar and slightly beaten egg in bowl. Add vanilla. In seprate bowl, sift dry ingredients, alternately with milk. Add chocolate and nuts.

Form into roll. Wrap in wax paper or plastic wrap. Refrigerate. When ready to bake, preheat oven to 350°. Slice thinly. Bake for about 10 minutes. Yields 40 cookies.

How can I tell if my butter is close to room temperature? Stick an instant-read thermometer into the center to see if it is at 65° to 67°. Or press the wrapped butter gently with your fingers. If this leaves an indentation and the butter is still firm, it's ready. Or see if you can bend the stick with your hands; it should still feel firm.

Chocolate Chip Cookies

½ cup butter at room temperature
¼ cup packed brown sugar
½ cup sugar
1 egg, well beaten
1 cup flour
½ teaspoon baking soda
1 (8 ounce) package semi-sweet chocolate chips
½ cup chopped nuts (optional)
1 teaspoon vanilla

Preheat oven to 375°. Cream butter in bowl. Add brown sugar and sugar gradually while creaming until light and fluffy. Add egg and mix well.

Sift flour once. Measure. Sift again with ½ teaspoon salt and baking soda. Combine mixtures thoroughly. Add chocolate chips, nuts and vanilla. Drop teaspoonfuls of mixture onto cookie sheet. Bake for 10 to 12 minutes. Yields 50 cookies.

Double Chocolate Cookies

6 egg whites
3 cups powdered sugar
¼ cup cocoa
3½ cups finely chopped pecans

Preheat oven to 325°. Beat egg whites in bowl until light and frothy. Fold powdered sugar and cocoa into egg whites and beat lightly. Fold in pecans.

Drop teaspoonfuls of dough onto sprayed, floured cookie sheet. Bake for about 20 minutes. Do not over bake and cool completely before removing from cookie sheet. Yields 3 dozen cookies.

Chocolate Pearls

2¼ cups flour
⅔ cup cocoa
1 teaspoon baking soda
1 cup (2 sticks) butter, softened
¾ cup sugar
⅔ cup firmly packed brown sugar
1 teaspoon vanilla
2 eggs
1 (12 ounce) package white chocolate chips

Preheat oven to 350°.

Combine flour, cocoa, baking soda and ½ teaspoon salt in bowl and set aside.

In separate bowl, beat butter, sugar, brown sugar and vanilla until creamy. Add eggs, one at a time, beating well after each addition. Gradually add dry ingredients and mix well. Stir in white chocolate chips and mix well.

Drop rounded tablespoonfuls of dough onto cookie sheet and bake for 9 to 10 minutes. Place on wire rack to cool. Store in an airtight container. Yields 3 to 4 dozen cookies.

Use pure extracts, not imitation. It really does make a difference.

Pixies

1 cup (2 sticks) butter, softened
1 cup crunchy peanut butter
1 cup sugar
1 cup packed brown sugar
2 eggs
2¼ cups flour
1 teaspoon baking soda
1 (6 ounce) package milk chocolate chips
¾ cup chopped pecans

Preheat oven to 350°.

Cream butter, peanut butter, sugar, brown sugar and eggs in bowl and beat well. Add flour and baking soda and mix well. Stir in chocolate chips and pecans.

Drop teaspoonfuls of dough onto sprayed cookie sheet. With spoon dipped in water, flatten each cookie slightly. Bake for 12 to 15 minutes and cool. Store in airtight container. Yields 3 dozen cookies.

For most recipes, it is best that all ingredients be at or close to room temperature. (However, some recipes do call for cold ingredients like piecrust and other pastries.)

Crunchy Double Chip Cookies

1⅓ cups sugar
1 cup (2 sticks) butter, softened
2 eggs
2 teaspoons vanilla
1¾ cups flour
1 teaspoon baking powder
½ teaspoon baking soda
8 cups crushed corn flakes
1 (6 ounce) package milk chocolate chips
1 (6 ounce) package peanut butter chips

Preheat oven to 350°.

Combine sugar, butter, eggs and vanilla in bowl and beat well. Stir in flour, ¼ teaspoon salt, baking powder and baking soda; mix well. Add crushed corn flakes, chocolate chips and peanut butter chips and mix well (batter will be thick).

Drop tablespoonfuls of dough onto cookie sheets and bake for 12 to 15 minutes. Cool and wire rack before storing. Yields 5 dozen cookies.

The Nestle Company introduced chocolate morsels in 1939.

The Best Chocolate Chip Cookie

¾ cup shortening
1½ cups packed brown sugar
2 tablespoons milk
2 teaspoons vanilla
1 egg, slightly beaten
1¾ cups flour
⅔ teaspoon baking soda
1 cup semi-sweet chocolate chips
1 cup chopped pecans

Preheat oven to 375°.

Cream shortening, brown sugar, milk and vanilla in large bowl and blend until creamy. Stir in egg and mix well. Add flour, ½ teaspoon salt and baking soda to creamed mixture and stir until they blend well. Add chocolate chips and pecans and mix well.

Drop rounded tablespoonfuls of dough onto cookie sheet. Bake for 10 minutes for chewy cookie and 11 to 13 minutes for a crisp cookie. Let cookies cool and store in an airtight container. Yields 3 dozen cookies.

Chocolate chip cookies were accidentally invented in 1930 by Massachusetts innkeeper Ruth Wakefield. Because she was out of baker's chocolate, she chopped up a bar of semisweet chocolate as a substitute, thinking the chocolate would melt into the dough as the cookies baked. They didn't and the result was a batch of delicious cookies studded with bits of chocolate – the original Toll House cookies named for the inn. The recipe continues to be published on Nestle's chocolate chips today.

Chocolate-Oat Cookies

1 cup (2 stick) butter, softened
1⅔ cups sugar
2 eggs
2 teaspoons vanilla
¾ teaspoon baking soda
1½ cups flour
3 tablespoons cocoa
1 teaspoon ground cinnamon
2½ cups quick-cooking oats
1 cup chopped pecans

Preheat oven to 350°. Combine butter, sugar, eggs and vanilla in bowl and beat until mixture is creamy. In separate bowl, combine baking soda, ½ teaspoon salt, flour, cocoa and cinnamon and mix well.

Stir in oats and pecans and drop teaspoonfuls of dough onto cookie sheets and bake for about 16 to 18 minutes. Remove cookies to wire rack to cool. Store in an airtight container. Yields 4 to 5 dozen cookies.

If you are uncertain about the freshness of eggs, cover them with a few inches of water. If eggs sink to the bottom of the container and lay horizontally, they are okay. If they sink, but stand on their ends or they float, discard them.

Chocolate Chip Peanut Butter Cookies

1 cup (2 sticks) butter softened
1½ cups sugar
1 cup packed brown sugar
2 eggs, beaten
1 cup chunky peanut butter
3 cups flour
1 teaspoon baking soda
1 teaspoon baking powder
1 cup chocolate chips
1 cup peanut butter chips

Preheat oven to 350°. Combine butter, sugar and brown sugar in bowl and beat until creamy. Add eggs one at a time and beat well after each addition. Fold in peanut butter and mix well.

In separate bowl, combine flour, baking soda, baking powder and ¼ teaspoon salt. Stir dry ingredients into butter mixture and mix well. Fold in chocolate chips and peanut butter chips; mix well.

Drop tablespoonfuls of batter onto sprayed cookie sheet and bake for 12 to 14 minutes or until cookies turn golden brown. Cool before storing. Yields 4 to 5 dozen cookies.

Store brown sugar in the freezer to keep it from hardening.

Hello Dollies

1½ cups graham cracker crumbs
1 (6 ounce) package chocolate chips
1 cup flaked coconut
1¼ cups chopped pecans
1 (14 ounce) can sweetened condensed milk

Preheat oven to 350°. Sprinkle cracker crumbs in 9 x 9-inch square pan. Layer chocolate chips, coconut and pecans. Pour sweetened condensed milk over top of layered ingredients. Bake for 25 to 30 minutes. Cool and cut into squares. Yields 9 squares.

Cowboy Cookies

2 cups flour
1 teaspoon baking soda
½ teaspoon baking powder
1 cup (2 sticks) butter, softened
1 cup sugar
1 cup packed brown sugar
2 eggs
1 teaspoon vanilla
2 cups quick-cooking oats
1 (6 ounce) package chocolate chips
1 cup chopped pecans

Preheat oven to 350°. Combine flour, baking soda, baking powder and ½ teaspoon salt in bowl and set aside.

In separate bowl, cream butter, sugar, brown sugar, eggs and vanilla until fluffy. Add flour mixture and mix well. Add oats, chocolate chips and pecans and mix well.

Drop teaspoonfuls of dough onto sprayed cookie sheet and bake for about 15 minutes. Yields 4 dozen cookies.

Sesame Balls

2 cups flour
1 cup sugar
1½ teaspoons baking powder
¾ cup shortening
2 egg yolks
¼ cup milk
1 teaspoon almond extract
½ cup sesame seeds

Preheat oven to 350°. Combine flour, sugar, baking powder and ⅛ teaspoon salt in bowl. Cut in shortening until mixture resembles coarse crumbs. Add egg yolks, milk and almond extract and mix until dough holds together.

Shape dough in 1-inch balls, roll in sesame seeds to coat completely. Place onto sprayed cookie sheet. Bake for 12 to 15 minutes or until cookies are light brown. Yields 3 dozen balls.

Old-Fashioned Butter Balls

¾ cup (1½ stick) butter, softened
1 cup packed brown sugar
1 egg, lightly beaten
1 teaspoon vanilla
2 cups flour
1½ teaspoons baking powder
½ cup sugar
1½ cups whole almonds

Preheat oven to 400°. Beat butter and brown sugar in bowl; add egg and vanilla. Gradually add flour, baking powder and ½ teaspoon salt and mix well. Using 1 level tablespoon at a time, form dough into balls and roll into sugar.

Place balls on sprayed cookie sheets and press whole almonds in center of each ball. Bake for 10 to 12 minutes. Transfer balls to wire racks to cool completely. Yields 4 to 5 dozen balls.

Chocolate Robins

½ cup flour
¼ cup butter at room temperature
2 ounces dark chocolate, melted
2 eggs
1 cup sugar
½ cup chopped nuts
1 teaspoon vanilla

Preheat oven to 350°. Sift flour once. Add ½ teaspoon salt and sift again. Place butter in bowl and cream until soft. Add warm melted chocolate and stir until thoroughly blended.

In separate bowl, beat eggs until very light and fluffy. Add sugar, small amount at a time, beating after each addition. Add egg mixture to chocolate mixture and fold in flour, nuts and vanilla.

Bake in sprayed 7 x 11-inch baking pan for 25 to 30 minutes. Cool and cut into squares. Yields 20 squares.

Butter should be just below room temperature (65° to 67°) for most recipes. Set it out for 15 to 30 minutes before use. However, if the recipe calls for cold butter, leave it in the refrigerator until you are ready to add it or you may not get the desired results, especially with piecrust and other pastry. It's often helpful to slice the butter ahead of time and put it back into the refrigerator so it will be well chilled.

Fig Newtons

½ cup butter at room temperature
1½ cups sugar
1 egg, well beaten
½ cup milk
1 teaspoon vanilla
3 cups flour
3 teaspoons baking powder
1 cup dried figs, chopped

Preheat oven to 400°. Cream butter and 1 cup sugar in bowl. Add egg and beat until light. Mix milk and vanilla. Sift ½ teaspoon salt, flour and baking powder and add alternately with milk to creamed mixture. Blend well.

Roll out ⅛ inch thick on slightly floured board in rectangle. Put figs in saucepan with remaining sugar and 1 cup boiling water. Boil for 5 minutes. Cool.

Spread cooked mixture over half of dough. Cover with remaining half of dough. Cut in oblong pieces. Bake for 12 to 15 minutes. Yields 20 cookies.

"Plump up" dried fruits or raisins before adding to a mixture by pouring boiling water over them and soak them for about 30 minutes. Drain and dry completely with paper towels.

Date Bars

1 cup walnuts, chopped
1 cup pitted dates, chopped
1 cup powdered sugar
2 eggs, beaten
1 tablespoon lemon juice
¼ cup flour
1 tablespoon melted butter
Powdered sugar, for serving

Preheat oven to 350°. Combine nuts, dates, powdered sugar and eggs. Mix well. Add remaining ingredients and ½ teaspoon salt in bowl and mix thoroughly.

Spread evenly in sprayed 7 x 11-inch pan. Bake for 20 to 25 minutes. While hot, cut into strips or bars and roll in powdered sugar. Yields 20 bars.

Blueberry Squares

2 cups flour
4 teaspoons baking powder
5 tablespoons butter, melted and cooled
⅔ cup milk
1½ cups blueberries
½ cup sugar
½ teaspoon ground cinnamon

Preheat oven to 375°. Mix flour, baking powder and ¼ teaspoon salt. Add butter and milk. Mix lightly and pour at once into sprayed shallow pan.

Press down until soft dough is about ⅔ inch thick. Mix blueberries with sugar and cinnamon. Quickly spread mixture on dough. Bake for 12 minutes. Cut in squares and serve fresh with butter. Yields 20 squares.

Raspberry Bars

1½ cups flour
1¼ cups old-fashioned oats
½ cup finely chopped almonds
½ cup sugar
⅓ cup packed brown sugar
¼ cup baking soda
¾ cup (1½ sticks) butter
1 cup raspberry jam

Preheat oven to 350°.

Combine flour, oats, almonds, sugar, brown sugar, baking soda and ¼ teaspoon salt in large bowl.

In separate bowl, beat butter and flour mixture on low speed until mixture is crumbly. Transfer two-thirds of oat mixture into sprayed, floured 9-inch square baking pan. Press firmly into even crust using your fingers and bake for 20 minutes.

Spread jam evenly over hot crust, then sprinkle remaining oat mixture over top. Continue baking until jam bubbles around edges and top is golden brown, about 30 minutes. Let cool completely before cutting into bars and removing from pan. Yields 25 bars.

Use a kitchen timer to make sure you mix for and bake for the correct amount of time.

Chewy Bars

3 eggs, beaten
1 (16 ounce) box light brown sugar
1 teaspoon vanilla
½ cup (1 stick) butter, melted, slightly cooled
2 cups flour
2 teaspoons baking powder
1½ cups chopped pecans

Preheat oven to 350°. Combine eggs, brown sugar, vanilla and butter in bowl and mix well. Gradually add flour and baking powder and mix well. Fold in pecans.

Spread batter into sprayed, floured 9 x 13-inch baking pan. Bake for about 35 minutes. Bars are done when toothpick is inserted in center comes out clean. If center is sticky, bake for additional 4 to 5 minutes. Cool and cut into bars. Yields 15 to 20 bars.

Butterscotch Squares

¼ cup butter at room temperature
1½ cups packed brown sugar, divided
2 eggs
1½ cups flour
⅓ cup whipping cream
½ cup chopped walnuts

Preheat oven to 350°. Cream butter in bowl. Add ¾ cup packed brown sugar and cream thoroughly. Add 1 egg and beat well. Mix flour and ½ teaspoon salt and add to first mixture alternately with cream.

Spread ⅛ inch thick on cookie sheets. Brush with remaining egg and sprinkle with remaining brown sugar mixed with nuts. Bake for 15 to 20 minutes. Cut into 2-inch squares while still hot. Yields 20 squares.

Almond-Butter Bars

1 cup (2 sticks) butter, softened
2 cups sugar
3 eggs, beaten
2 cups flour
1½ teaspoons baking powder
3 teaspoons almond extract
½ cup finely chopped slivered almonds

Preheat oven to 350°.

Combine butter and sugar in bowl and beat until fluffy. Add eggs and beat thoroughly.

In separate bowl, combine flour and baking powder and gradually add to sugar mixture. Fold in almond extract and almonds and mix well.

Spread dough into sprayed, floured 9 x 13-inch baking pan and bake for 35 minutes. Cool and cut into bars. Yields 15 to 20 bars.

TIP: *Be sure to use butter. There is no substitute for the real thing in this recipe.*

I forgot to take the eggs out of the refrigerator! How do I get them to room temperature fast? Put the eggs in bowl of warm, not hot, water for 2 minutes only. Stir the eggs so they do not begin to cook. If they are still cold, repeat for another 2 minutes. Dry the eggs with a towel before cracking them.

Butter Pecan Turtle Bars

2 cups flour
1¾ cup packed light brown sugar, divided
1¼ cups (2½ sticks) butter, softened, divided
1½ cups coarsely chopped pecans
¼ cup (½ stick) butter
5 (1 ounce) squares semi-sweet chocolate

Preheat oven to 350°. Combine flour, ¾ cup packed brown sugar and ½ cup (1 stick) butter in large bowl and blend until crumbly. Pat mixture firmly into sprayed, floured 9 x 13-inch baking pan and sprinkle pecans over unbaked crust. Set aside.

Combine remaining brown sugar and 6 tablespoons (¾ stick) butter in small saucepan over medium heat and stir constantly until mixture boils. Cook and stir for 1 minute.

Drizzle caramel sauce over pecans and crust. Bake for 18 minutes or until caramel layer bubbles. Remove from oven and cool.

Melt chocolate squares and ¼ cup (½ stick) butter in saucepan and stir until smooth. Pour over bars and spread evenly. Cool and cut into bars. Store in refrigerator. Yields 15 to 20 bars.

Prehistoric peoples made sweet treats with honey. Honey also acted as a preservative.

Pecan Pie Squares

Crust:

3 cups flour
1¼ cups (2½ sticks) butter, softened
⅓ cup sugar

Preheat oven to 350°.

Blend flour, butter, sugar and ¾ teaspoon salt in bowl. Press dough into sprayed, floured 12 x 18-inch jellyroll pan and bake for 25 minutes or until crust browns.

Filling:

4 eggs, beaten
1½ cups packed brown sugar
1½ cups light corn syrup
3 tablespoons butter, melted
1½ teaspoons vanilla
2½ cups chopped pecans

Combine eggs, brown sugar, corn syrup, butter and vanilla in bowl and mix well. Spread pecans over crust, then pour egg mixture over baked layer and spread evenly.

Bake for about 25 minutes more or until filling sets. Cool and cut into squares. Yields 24 to 30 squares.

Apricot Squares

½ cup (1 stick) plus 6 teaspoons butter, softened
1 cup sugar, divided
2 eggs
1 cup flour
1 teaspoon baking powder
9 ripe apricots
3 teaspoons butter
3 tablespoons brandy
1 teaspoon grated orange peel

Preheat oven to 350°. Cream ½ cup (1 stick) butter and half sugar in bowl. Add eggs and beat until very light. In separate bowl, sift flour with baking powder and stir into creamed mixture.

Pour into sprayed, floured square cake pan. Press apricot halves, pitted but not peeled into batter skin-side down. Place in each half ⅓ teaspoon butter and an equal amount of brandy.

Sprinkle over all remaining sugar and orange peel mixed. Bake for 30 minutes and cut into squares. Yields 9 squares.

Always use the freshest ingredients available to get the best results. Be sure to check expiration dates, particularly leavening such as yeast, baking soda and baking powder. Be sure dairy and other perishable products are fresh.

Zesty Lemon Squares

1¼ cups (2½ sticks) butter, softened
½ cup sugar
½ cup packed brown sugar
1½ cups flour
1 teaspoon baking powder
1 cup quick-cooking oats
1 (14 ounce) can sweetened condensed milk
½ cup lemon juice
1 egg, slightly beaten

Preheat oven to 350°.

Beat butter, sugar and brown sugar in bowl until creamy. Stir in flour, baking powder and oats and mix until mixture is crumbly. Spread half mixture into sprayed, floured 9 x 13-inch baking pan; pat mixture down.

In separate bowl, combine sweetened condensed milk, lemon juice and egg and mix until blended well. Sprinkle with remaining crumb mixture and bake for 25 minutes. Cool at room temperature for 1 hour and cut into squares. Yields 15 to 20 squares.

Always mix ingredients for the time shown in the recipe or to the consistency described in the recipe. This will be different from recipe to recipe. Do not over-mix or over-beat.

Praline Squares

1½ cups flour
½ cup powdered sugar
1½ cups (3 stick) butter, softened
1 cup chopped pecans
1¼ cups light corn syrup
1 cup packed brown sugar
¼ cup (½ stick) butter, softened
4 eggs
2 cups coarsely chopped pecans
1 teaspoon vanilla
1 (12 ounce) package butterscotch chips

Preheat oven to 325°. Combine flour and powdered sugar in large bowl and cut in 1½ cups butter. Stir in 1 cup chopped pecans and press mixture into sprayed, floured 9 x 13-inch baking pan. Bake for 20 minutes.

Combine syrup, brown sugar and ¼ cup butter in medium saucepan. Bring mixture to a boil, stirring constantly. Remove from heat and let cool slightly.

Beat eggs on low speed for about 2 minutes. Continue beating, slowly adding warm mixture. Stir in 2 cups pecans and vanilla. Pour filling into crust and sprinkle with butterscotch chips. Bake for 35 minutes or until center is set. When cool; cut into squares. Yields 20 to 24 squares.

Southern Chess Squares

1 cup (2 sticks) butter
1 (16 ounce) box light brown sugar
½ cup sugar
4 eggs
1 teaspoon vanilla
2 cups flour
1 teaspoon baking powder
1 cup chopped pecans
Sifted powder sugar

Preheat oven to 325°.

Heat butter and brown sugar in saucepan until butter melts, stirring well. Remove from heat and stir in sugar, eggs and vanilla and beat well.

Combine flour and baking powder in bowl; stir in butter-sugar mixture, mixing well. Stir in pecans and spread into sprayed, floured 10 x 15-inch jellyroll pan. Bake for 35 to 40 minutes

Let stand at room temperature for about 15 to 20 minutes; sprinkle with sifted powder sugar while squares are still warm. Cut into squares to serve. Yields 24 to 32 squares.

Why is it important to have eggs at room temperature? Typically, in a recipe calling for a mixture of creamed butter and sugar, the beating of eggs 1 at a time into the mixture creates an emulsion (a mixture of two things that do not usually mix well, such as oil and vinegar). A good emulsion results in a batter that will not curdle or seep liquid; this can happen if the eggs are cold when added and the results will not be good.

Caramel Treats

1 cup (2 sticks) butter, softened
1 (16 ounce) box dark brown sugar
2 eggs, beaten
1⅔ cups flour
2 teaspoons baking powder
2 teaspoons vanilla
2 cups chopped pecans
Sifted powdered sugar

Preheat oven to 350°.

Combine butter and brown sugar in large saucepan and melt. Quickly remove from heat and cool. Add eggs one at a time and beat well after each addition. Add flour, baking powder, ⅛ teaspoon salt and vanilla and mix well. Stir in pecans.

Pour batter into sprayed, floured 9 x 13-inch baking pan and bake for 25 to 30 minutes. Treats are done when toothpick is inserted in center and comes out clean.

Cool and dust with powdered sugar. Cut into squares. Yields 15 to 20 squares.

TIP: *Be sure to use butter. There is no substitute for the real thing in this recipe.*

Use the correct pan size for the recipe to get the results you want.

Brownies

1 cup sugar
1½ tablespoons cocoa
¼ cup butter, melted
1 egg
½ cup flour
1 teaspoon vanilla
½ cup chopped nuts, optional

Preheat oven to 350°. Cream sugar, cocoa and butter in bowl
and add remaining ingredients, mixing well. Spread dough in
sprayed, floured 9 x 13-inch pan. Bake for 30 minutes. Cut into
pieces while warm. Yields 20 squares.

Bangor Brownies

1 cup flour
1 teaspoon baking powder
¼ cup melted butter
⅓ cup molasses
1 egg
2 ounces dark chocolate, melted
1 cup nuts, chopped

Preheat oven to 375°. Sift flour, baking powder and pinch of salt
in bowl. In separate bowl, mix remaining ingredients in order given
and beat thoroughly. Combine two mixtures.

Spread mixture evenly in 9-inch cake pan that has been lined
with sprayed paper or parchment paper. Bake for about 15 minutes.
Remove paper from cake as soon as it is taken from the oven and
cut into small squares or strips with sharp knife. Yields 16 squares.

Cashew Brownies

18 caramels
6 tablespoons (¾ stick) butter
2 tablespoons milk
¾ cup sugar
2 eggs, beaten
1 teaspoon vanilla
1 cup flour
½ teaspoon baking powder
1 cup chopped cashews

Preheat oven to 350°. Combine caramels, butter and milk in saucepan and stir constantly over low heat until caramels melt and mixture is smooth. Remove from heat and stir in sugar. Cool several minutes, then add eggs and vanilla.

Combine flour and baking powder in bowl. Stir in caramel mixture and blend. Fold in cashews.

Spoon batter into sprayed, floured 9-inch square baking pan and bake for about 25 minutes. Brownies are done when toothpick is inserted in center and comes out clean. Cool on wire rack and cut into bars. Yields 12 to 15 brownies.

Brownies were first mentioned in 1897 and soon became very popular.

Apple Brownies

½ cup (1 stick) butter, melted
1 cup sugar
1 egg
1 cup flour
½ teaspoon baking powder
½ teaspoon baking soda
1 teaspoon ground cinnamon
2 small apples, peeled, finely chopped
½ cup coarsely chopped walnuts

Preheat oven to 350°. Cream butter, sugar and egg in bowl and beat until creamy. Stir in flour, ¼ teaspoon salt, baking powder, baking soda and cinnamon and mix until they blend well.

Fold in apples and walnuts, mixing well. Spoon into sprayed, floured 9-inch square baking pan and bake for 40 to 45 minutes. Let cool completely before cutting in squares. Yields 16 brownies.

Blonde Brownies

¾ cup (1½ sticks) butter, softened
1¾ cups packed light brown sugar
3 eggs, lightly beaten
1 teaspoon vanilla
2¼ cups flour
2½ teaspoons baking powder
1 (12 ounce) package chocolate chips

Preheat oven to 350°. Combine butter and brown sugar in large bowl until creamy. Stir in eggs and vanilla and mix thoroughly. Gradually add flour, baking powder and ½ teaspoon salt a little at a time and beat after each addition. Stir in chocolate chips.

Pour into sprayed, floured 9 x 13-inch baking pan and bake for about 22 minutes or until top springs back when touched. Cool in pan and cut into squares. Yields 15 brownies.

Butterscotch Brownies

3 cups packed brown sugar
1 cup (2 sticks) butter, softened
3 eggs
3 cups flour
2 tablespoons baking powder
1½ cups chopped pecans
1 cup flaked coconut

Preheat oven to 350°. Combine brown sugar and butter in bowl and beat until fluffy; add eggs and blend well.

In separate bowl, sift flour, baking powder and ½ teaspoon salt. Add flour mixture to sugar-butter mixture 1 cup at a time, mixing well after each addition.

Add pecans and coconut and spread batter into sprayed, floured 10 x 15-inch baking pan. Bake for 20 to 25 minutes. (Batter will be hard to spread.)

Glaze:

½ cup packed brown sugar
⅓ cup evaporated milk
½ cup (1 stick) butter
1 cup powdered sugar
½ teaspoon vanilla

Combine ½ cup packed brown sugar, evaporated milk, butter and ⅛ teaspoon salt in saucepan; bring mixture to a boil. Remove from heat and cool slightly. Add powdered sugar and vanilla and beat until smooth. Spread over cooked brownies and cut into squares. Yields 20 to 24 brownies.

Ultimate Fudgy Brownies

5 (1 ounce) squares semi-sweet chocolate, chopped
2 (1 ounce) squares unsweetened chocolate, chopped
½ cup (1 stick) butter
3 tablespoons cocoa
1½ cups sugar
3 large eggs
2 teaspoons vanilla
1 cup flour

Preheat oven to 350°.

Melt chocolates, butter and cocoa in saucepan while stirring constantly. Let mixture cool slightly.

Whisk sugar, eggs, vanilla and ½ teaspoon salt in large bowl. Whisk in melted chocolate mixture until smooth. Stir in flour and mix until blended well.

Pour into sprayed, floured 8-inch square baking pan and bake for 35 minutes or until toothpick inserted in center comes out clean.

Let cool completely on wire rack for about 2 hours before cutting into squares and removing brownies from pan. Yields 3 dozen small brownies.

Brownies and bars are much easier to remove from the pan if you line the pan with foil. Here's an easy method. Turn the pan upside down and cover it with a big enough piece to cover the sides as well as the bottom of the pan. Be sure to place the foil shiny side down. Press the foil around the pan, carefully remove it and turn the pan over. Then fit the shaped foil, shiny side up, into the pan. Use a paper towel to smooth it down.

Rum-Frosted Brownies

1 cup (2 sticks) butter
4 (1 ounce) unsweetened chocolate
3 eggs
2 cups sugar
2 teaspoons vanilla
1 cup flour
1 cup chopped pecans

Preheat oven at 350°. Melt butter and chocolate in saucepan and set aside to cool.

Beat eggs, sugar and vanilla in large bowl. Stir in chocolate mixture and gradually fold in flour. Stir in pecans. Spread batter into sprayed, floured 9 x 13-inch baking pan and bake for 30 minutes or until top feels firm to the touch. Cool completely. Yields 20 to 24 brownies.

Rum Frosting:

½ cup (1 stick) butter, softened
1 (16 ounce) package powdered sugar
3½ tablespoons rum
6 (1 ounce) semi-sweet chocolate
2 tablespoons butter
½ cup chopped pecans

Combine butter, powdered sugar and rum in bowl and spread over cooled brownies. Melt chocolate and butter in saucepan and spread evenly over powdered sugar mixture.

Sprinkle pecans over chocolate. Let stand until chocolate becomes firm, then cut into bars. Yields 15 brownies.

TIP: You may substitute rum with 3 teaspoons milk and 1½ teaspoons rum flavoring for 3½ tablespoons rum.

Desserts
&
Candies

**Delicious delights that remind
you of the old home place!**

Desserts & Candies Contents

Desserts

Custards, puddings, and candies are at the heart of this chapter. There are two major types of custards: those that are prepared on the stove (such as the soft custard), and those that are baked (such as the baked custard). For each, the key lies in cooking them just until they are done and no further.

For the stovetop custards, the easiest method is to test whether or not the custard will coat a spoon. Though that may sound a bit vague, it means something rather precise. When cooking custard in double boiler, use a wooden spoon. As soon as the mixture starts to thicken, dip the spoon in the custard and pull it out. Draw a line in the custard with a finger or spoon. If that line stays and doesn't fill in with custard immediately, the custard is done. To see more of a contrast, try this test as soon as the custard starts cooking. The custard should be runny and the line should fill in immediately.

For baked custards, there are two ways to check for doneness. Insert a metal knife slightly off center in the custard. If it comes out clean, the custard should be done; or jiggle the custard pan a bit. If the center (an area no larger than a quarter) is wobbly, but the rest of the custard seems firm, the custard is done. Overcooked custard will have the taste of sweet scrambled eggs. There is a small window in which to remove the custard from heat, because the eggs will thicken when they reach 160° and begin to cook when they get to 180°.

Puddings are much less temperamental than custards. For any bread puddings, the only trick is to make sure that there is enough liquid for the bread. If the bread is especially stale, it may be necessary to add additional milk or butter to ensure that the pudding doesn't dry out. Other than that, puddings are delightfully easy. Just preheat the oven, combine the ingredients, and bake.

Chocolate Souffle

2 tablespoons butter
3 tablespoons flour
1 cup milk
½ cup sugar
3 ounces dark chocolate, melted and cooled slightly
3 eggs, separated
1 teaspoon vanilla, or 1 vanilla bean, scraped

Preheat oven to 350°. Melt butter in saucepan and blend in flour. Add milk slowly and bring to a boil, stirring constantly. Add sugar and ½ teaspoon salt. Add chocolate to mixture. Cool.

Add egg yolks and beat until light. Add vanilla or vanilla beans. Beat egg whites until stiff. Fold in egg whites gently, deflating as little as possible.

Turn onto sprayed souffle dish. Set in pan of hot water. Bake for 40 to 45 minutes. Serve immediately with whipped cream if desired. Serves 6.

Prepare your baking pans ahead of time so they will be ready to use when the mixture is placed in them. Be sure to prepare the pans according to the directions in the recipe.

Apricot Souffle

2 tablespoons butter
3 tablespoons flour
1 cup milk
¼ cup sugar
¼ cup apricot jam
3 eggs, separated

Preheat oven to 350°. Melt butter in saucpan and blend in flour. Add milk slowly and bring to a boil, stirring constantly. Add sugar and ½ teaspoon salt. Add apricot jam to mixture. Cool.

Add egg yolks and beat until light. Beat egg whites until stiff. Fold in egg whites gently, deflating as little as possible. Turn onto sprayed souffle dish. Set in pan of hot water. Bake for 40 to 45 minutes. Serve immediately with whipped cream if desired. Serves 6.

Bread Pudding

1½ cups stale bread or croissants, cut into ½ -nch to 1-inch cubes
3 cups hot milk
2 eggs, beaten
⅔ cup sugar
1 tablespoon butter
½ teaspoon vanilla
½ teaspoon ground cinnamon
½ cup apples, peeled and diced
¼ cup raisins
¼ cup walnuts, chopped
Whipped cream

Preheat oven to 350°. Combine bread, milk, eggs, sugar, ¼ teaspoon salt and butter in bowl. Mix well, then add vanilla, cinnamon, apples, raisins and nuts. Turn into sprayed 9-inch baking pan. Bake for 35 to 40 minutes or until firm. Serve with whipped cream. Serves 6.

Cherry Bread Pudding

1½ cups stale bread or croissants, cut into ½ inch to 1 inch cubes
3 cups hot milk
2 eggs, beaten
1 cup sugar
1 tablespoon butter
½ teaspoon vanilla
½ teaspoon ground cinnamon
1½ cups stoned, chopped cherries
¼ cup raisins
¼ cup walnuts, chopped
Whipped cream

Preheat oven to 350°.

Combine bread, milk, eggs, sugar, ¼ teaspoon salt and butter in bowl. Mix well, then add vanilla, cinnamon, cherries, raisins and nuts.

Turn into sprayed 9-inch baking pan. Bake for 35 to 40 minutes or until firm. Serve with whipped cream. Serves 6.

Position the oven rack before preheating the oven. Most baked goods do well on a rack placed in the middle of the oven to allow for air circulation. However, when using a gas oven, you may wish to place breads and pies on a lower rack.

Bread Pudding with Whiskey Sauce

3 tablespoons butter
1 loaf French bread
1 quart milk
3 eggs
2 cups sugar
2 tablespoons vanilla
1 cup raisins

Preheat oven to 350°. Melt butter in 3-quart baking dish and cool. Soak bread in milk in bowl and crush with hands. Mix thoroughly. Add eggs, sugar, vanilla and raisins and stir well. Pour mixture over melted butter and bake for 55 to 60 minutes or until very firm.

Cool, cube pudding and pour into individual dessert dishes. When ready to serve, add Whiskey Sauce below.

Whiskey Sauce:

1 cup sugar
½ cup (1 stick) butter
1 egg, well beaten
Whiskey

Heat sugar and butter in double boiler until very hot and completely dissolved. Add egg, beating quickly so egg doesn't curdle. Cool and add whiskey to taste. Serves 18.

Cottage Pudding

¼ cup butter
¾ cup sugar
2 eggs
2¼ cups flour
3 teaspoons baking soda
¾ cup milk
1 teaspoon vanilla

Preheat oven to 400°. Cream butter, sugar and eggs in bowl. In seprate bowl, mix and sift flour, baking soda and ½ teaspoon salt. Add alternately with milk to first mixture. Add vanilla. Beat well.

Turn into sprayed baking pan or muffin pan to depth of 1 to 1½ inches. Bake for 20 to 25 minutes. Serve with Lemon Sauce (page 91). Serves 6.

Bread-and-Butter Pudding

⅓ cup raisins
5 thin slices stale bread
¼ cup butter, melted
2 eggs
⅔ cup sugar
2 cups milk
½ teaspoon vanilla
½ teaspoon ground cinnamon

Preheat oven to 375°. Line bottom of sprayed baking dish with raisins. Cut bread slices in 3 strips, crosswise. Dip each in melted butter and arrange on top of raisins.

Beat remaining ingredients in bowland pour over bread. Set dish in pan of hot water. Bake until bread is brown and knife blade inserted in center comes out clean, about 35 or 40 minutes. Serve plain or with cream. Serves 6.

Spiced Bread Pudding

1 cup toasted 1 inch chunks of bread or croissants
1 cup packed brown sugar
1 teaspoon baking soda
½ teaspoon ground cloves
½ teaspoon ground nutmeg
1 teaspoon ground cinnamon
1 cup buttermilk
1 cup raisins

Preheat oven to 325°. Combine bread, sugar, baking soda, cloves, nutmeg and cinnamon in bowl. Add buttermilk and raisins. Mix well. Turn into sprayed pudding dish. Bake for about 1 hour. Serves 4 to 6.

Rice Pudding

2 eggs, separated
½ cup sugar
2¼ cups milk
1 teaspoon vanilla
2 cups steamed rice
Dash ground nutmeg
Dash ground cinnamon

Preheat oven to 350°. Beat egg yolks in bowl. Add sugar, ½ teaspoon salt, milk, vanilla and rice. Stiffly beat egg whites and fold into mixture.

Turn into baking dish. Sprinkle with nutmeg and cinnamon. Bake for 45 minutes. Serves 6.

Old-Fashioned Rice Pudding

1 cup rice
1 quart milk
½ cup (1 stick) butter
5 eggs
¾ cup sugar
½ cup raisins
1 teaspoon vanilla
2 teaspoons ground cinnamon

Preheat oven to 350°. Combine rice, milk and butter in saucepan. Bring to a boil, cover and cook over low heat until rice is tender and absorbs most of milk.

Add eggs, sugar, raisins and vanilla to mixture and pour into sprayed 2-quart baking dish. Sprinkle cinnamon on top and bake for 25 minutes. Serves 12 to 14.

Tapioca Custard Pudding

⅓ cup minute tapioca
2 cups scalded milk (boiled and slightly cooled)
2 eggs, slightly beaten
½ cup sugar
1 tablespoon butter

Preheat oven to 325°. Add tapioca to milk and cook in double boiler over low heat for 30 minutes. Add eggs to sugar and 1 teaspoon salt. Pour gradually into hot mixture.

Turn into sprayed baking dish. Add butter. Put in pan of hot water. Bake for 30 minutes. One cup of almost any fruits or berries may be added. Serves 6.

Caramel Pudding

1 cup packed brown sugar
4 cups milk
¼ cup butter
4 eggs, separated
¼ cup cornstarch
1 cup sugar

Preheat oven to 350°. Bring brown sugar and milk to boiling point in saucepan over medium heat, stirring constantly. Add butter. Beat yolks and cornstarch in bowl and add to first mixture.

Cook, stirring constantly until thick. Turn into sprayed baking pan. Bake until brown. Beat egg whites with sugar and brush on top. Return to oven and brown top. Serves 6.

Butterscotch-Nut Pudding

2¼ cups milk
1½ cups packed brown sugar
3 tablespoons butter
3 egg yolks
6 tablespoons flour
½ cup nuts, chopped
Whipped cream

Preheat oven to 325°. Bring 1¾ cups milk in saucepan to a boil over medium heat. Add brown sugar and butter. Remove from heat, stirring until they dissolve.

Combine slightly beaten egg yolks with remaining milk in bowl. Mix with flour and ⅛ teaspoon salt. Add first milk mixture and nuts. Pour in sprayed baking pan. Cover and bake for 45 minutes. Serve with whipped cream. Serves 6.

Lemon-Sponge Pudding

1 cup sugar
1 tablespoon flour
2 eggs, separated
1 cup milk
Peel and juice of 1 lemon
2 tablespoons butter

Preheat oven to 350°. Sift sugar, flour and pinch of salt in bowl and blend with egg yolks. Add milk, lemon juice and peel, beating thoroughly. Melt butter and add to mixture.

Stiffly beat egg whites and fold them into mixture. Bake in baking dish set in pan of hot water for 45 minutes. Serve cold. Serves 6.

Peach Crisp Pudding

¼ cup butter at room temperature
½ cup sugar
4 cups bread cubes
2 cups diced peaches and juice
1 tablespoon freshly-squeezed lemon juice

Preheat oven to 375°. Cream butter and sugar in bowl. Add bread cubes to sugar mixture and blend well. Mix peaches and lemon juice with bread. Pour into sprayed baking pan or individual baking dishes and bake for 35 minutes.

Garnish with peaches and whipped cream if desired. Serve hot. Apricots or crushed pineapple may be substituted for peaches. Hot Lemon Sauce (page 91) goes well with this. Serves 6.

Peach Crumble Pudding

6 - 8 peaches, peeled and halved
¼ cup packed brown sugar
½ cup sifted flour
⅛ teaspoon ground nutmeg
¼ cup butter

Preheat oven to 350°. Place peaches in sprayed baking dish. Combine remaining ingredients in bowl, working together with fingertips to consistency of fine crumbs. Sprinkle over peaches. Bake for 25 to 30 minutes. Serve warm. Serves 6.

Roly-Poly Pudding

2 cups flour
4 teaspoons baking powder
5 tablespoons butter, divided
½ cup milk
5 tart apples, sliced
½ teaspoon ground cinnamon
½ teaspoon ground nutmeg
½ cup sugar

Preheat oven to 350°. Mix and sift flour, baking powder and 1 teaspoon salt in bowl. Rub in 3 tablespoons butter with fingertips. Add milk and mix to a soft dough.

Turn out on floured board and pat into oblong shape. Spread with remaining 2 tablespoons softened butter. Cover with layer of thinly sliced apples and sprinkle with cinnamon, nutmeg and sugar.

Roll like a jellyroll. Bake for 30 to 40 minutes. Slice 1 inch thick and serve hot with Lemon Sauce (page 91) or whipped cream. Serves 10.

Corn Flake Pudding

4 cups corn flakes
4 cups milk
2 eggs, slightly beaten
¼ cup molasses
¼ cup sugar
¼ teaspoon ground ginger
¼ teaspoon ground cinnamon
1 teaspoon vanilla
1 tablespoon butter

Preheat oven to 350°. Combine all ingredients and ½ teaspoon salt except butter in bowl Turn into sprayed baking dish. Dot with butter. Place dish in pan of water and put in oven. Bake for 45 minutes to 1 hour. Serves 8.

Grated Sweet Potato Pudding

3 cups grated raw sweet potatoes
½ cup sugar
½ cup maple syrup
1 cup milk
1 teaspoon ground nutmeg
2 tablespoons butter, melted
½ cup chopped nuts
2 eggs, well beaten

Preheat oven to 375°. Combine sweet potatoes, sugar, maple syrup, milk, nutmeg, butter, nuts and ½ teaspoon salt in bowl. Add eggs and pour into sprayed shallow baking pan. Bake for 50 to 60 minutes. Serves 6.

Sweet Potato Pudding

4 large sweet potatoes, peeled, finely shredded
1 cup buttermilk
2 (12 ounce) cans evaporated milk
2 cups sugar
1½ cups (3 sticks) butter, melted
1 teaspoon ground nutmeg
1 teaspoon ground cinnamon
1 teaspoon baking soda

Preheat oven to 350°. Place sweet potatoes in large, covered ovenproof dish. Pour buttermilk and evaporated milk over sweet potatoes immediately after shredding so they will not change color.

Stir in sugar, butter, nutmeg and cinnamon. Add baking soda and stir slightly. Bake for 1 hour 30 minutes. Serve hot. Serves 12.

Peach Crisp

1½ quarts peaches, peeled, sliced
½ cup sugar
Lemon juice
Ground nutmeg
Ground cinnamon
½ cup (1 stick) butter, melted
¾ cup self-rising flour
1 cup sugar

Preheat oven to 350°. Arrange peaches and sugar in 3-quart baking dish. Sprinkle lemon juice, nutmeg and cinnamon, as desired.

Mix butter, flour and sugar in bowl and spread topping over peaches. Bake for 30 to 35 minutes or until brown. Serve plain or with whipped cream or ice cream. Serves 8.

Peach Cobbler

2½ cups peeled sliced peaches
2 tablespoons granulated tapioca
¼ cup sugar
¼ teaspoon ground cinnamon
Dash ground nutmeg
1 tablespoon butter
Baking Powder Biscuit dough (page 239)

Preheat the oven to 400°. Empty peaches into shallow baking dish. Add tapioca and let stand for about 10 minutes.

Add sugar, ¼ teaspoon salt and spices. Mix well. Dot with butter. Roll biscuit dough to ¼ inch thickness. Prick and arrange over top of peach mixture.

Bake for about 30 minutes or until well brown. Apricots, blackberries, blueberries, black or red raspberries may be used instead of peaches. Serves 8.

Do not open the oven early in the baking process. It can create a draft and cause a sudden drop in the oven temperature. Do, however, check on the doneness before the time is up. For example, if a recipe says to bake for 40 to 45 minutes, check on the item when about 35 minutes have passed.

Apple Brown Betty

½ cup sugar
¼ teaspoon ground cinnamon
¼ teaspoon ground nutmeg
1½ cups bread in 1-inch cubes
3 cups sliced or chopped apples
¼ cup apple juice
Juice and peel of 1 lemon
3 tablespoons butter

Preheat oven to 350°. Mix sugar, spices and ½ teaspoon salt in bowl.
If apples are very tart, use additional sugar, up to 1 cup. Spray 1½-quart baking dish.

Put in one-third of bread, then half of apples. Sprinkle with half of sugar mixture. Repeat. Mix apple juice, lemon juice and peel; pour over casserole. Put on remaining crumbs and dot with butter.

Cover and bake for 1 hour 45 minutes. Serves 6.

TIP: Rhubarb, peaches, pineapple, bananas or cherries may be used instead of apples.

There is no substitute for butter in baking. Margarine, light butter and whipped butter contain water and do not have the right amount of fat for baking.

Apple Delights

2 cups flour
1½ teaspoons baking powder
¼ cup butter, cold
1 cup milk
1 egg, beaten
6 tart apples
Brown sugar

Preheat oven to 350°. Mix and sift flour, baking powder and ½ teaspoon salt in bowl. Cut in butter with knife. Add milk and egg and mix well. Drop tablespoons of batter into sprayed muffin cups.

Peel apples, cut in half and take out cores. Put on top of batter, cut-side up and fill holes with brown sugar. Bake for 25 minutes or until apples are tender. Serve hot with cream or sweetened whipped cream, dusted with ground cinnamon. Serves 6.

Baked goods began with simple breads. Cakes, cookies, pastries, biscuits all owe their beginning to bread.

Apple Crow's Nest

4 tart apples, cored, peeled, and sliced
4½ tablespoons butter, divided
¾ cup sugar, divided
2½ teaspoons ground cinnamon, divided
1 cup flour
2 teaspoons baking powder
¼ cup milk

Preheat oven to 350°. Arrange apples in sprayed pie pan and dot with 1½ tablespoons butter. Sprinkle with 1 tablespoon sugar and 1½ teaspoons cinnamon.

Sift flour, baking powder, ¼ teaspoon salt and ¼ cup sugar in bowl. Cut in remaining butter with knife or finger tips.

Add milk and mix to make a soft dough. Spread over apples. Bake until apples are tender, about 25 minutes.

Turn out upside down. Mix remaining sugar (7 tablespoons) and 1 teaspoon cinnamon and sprinkle over apples. Serve hot with whipped cream. Serves 6.

Baking powder and baking soda were invented in the 19th century.

Cranberry Roll

2½ cups flour
4 teaspoons baking powder
¼ cup sugar, plus 2 tablespoons
2 tablespoons cold butter, plus more for finishing
1 egg, beaten
¾ cup milk
2 cups cranberries, fresh or frozen

Preheat oven to 375°.

Mix and sift flour, baking powder,
1 teaspoon salt, and ¼ cup sugar in bowl. Work in butter with
finger tips.

Add egg and just enough milk, gradually, to make a soft dough.
Roll out on floured board to ½ inch thickness.

Spread surface generously with butter. Cover with cranberries.
Sprinkle with remaining sugar.

Roll as a jellyroll. Put in sprayed baking pan. Brush top and
sides with butter. Bake until it begins to brown, about 15 minutes.

Reduce heat to 350° and bake for 45 minutes longer. Slice
1 inch thick and serve hot with Lemon Sauce (page 91). Serves 6.

Peach Basket Turnover

2 eggs, separated, beaten
1 cup sugar
1 cup flour
1 teaspoon baking powder
1 teaspoon vanilla
1 cup packed brown sugar
2 tablespoons butter
1½ cups peeled, sliced ripe peaches
Whipped cream

Preheat oven to 350°. Beat yolks with sugar in bowl until light. Fold in stiffly beaten egg whites. In seprate bowl, mix and sift flour, baking powder and ¼ teaspoon salt. Add to first mixture and mix thoroughly, but gently. Add vanilla.

Cream brown sugar and butter in bowl. Add peaches and ¼ teaspoon salt and place in sprayed shallow baking pan. Pour batter over peaches. Bake for 45 minutes.

Turn out upside down. Serve hot with whipped cream. Serves 6.

Work quickly when preparing recipes for baking. Many ingredients begin to work together immediately. Baking powder, for example, begins its leavening action as soon as it is moistened. Make sure your pans and other equipment are ready, your ingredients are ready (at room temperature for most recipes), and your oven will be at the right temperature. Pre-measuring your ingredients will also help you work quickly.

Cream Cheese Torte

¼ cup butter
25 graham crackers, crumbled
½ pound cream cheese
½ pound cottage cheese
1½ cups sour cream
4 eggs, separated
½ cup sugar
1 teaspoon vanilla

Preheat oven to 375°. Melt butter in saucepan. Add cracker crumbs, reserving 3 teaspoons. Line sprayed 9 x 13-inch baking dish with crumbs.

Blend cream cheese and cottage cheese in bowl. Add sour cream and mix well. Add egg yolks, sugar, pinch of salt and vanilla, beat thoroughly.

Stiffly beat egg whites and gently fold them into mixture. Turn into baking dish. Sprinkle reserved crumbs over top.

Bake for 35 minutes. Cool before serving. Excellent with fresh berries or other fruit. Serves 12.

Have a cooling rack ready and easy to get to when removing items from the oven. Have dry oven mitts or hot pads ready as well.

Pavlova

3 large egg whites
1 cup sugar
1 teaspoon vanilla
2 teaspoons white vinegar
3 tablespoons cornstarch
Whipped cream
Fresh fruit

Preheat oven to 300°.

Beat egg whites in bowl until stiff and add 3 tablespoons cold water. Beat again and add sugar very gradually while beating. Continue beating slowly and add vanilla, vinegar and cornstarch.

On parchment-covered baking sheet, draw 9-inch circle and mound mixture within circle. Bake for 45 minutes. Leave in oven to cool.

To serve, peel paper from bottom while sliding Pavlova onto serving plate. Cover with whipped cream and top with assortment of fresh fruit such as kiwi, strawberries, blueberries, etc. Serves 12.

Pavlovas are named for the famous Russian ballerina, Anna Pavlova. The meringue dessert was invented about the time of her tour of Australia and New Zealand in 1926. Both countries claim credit for this sweet treat.

Strawberry Pavlova

5 egg whites
1¾ cups sugar, divided
1 teaspoon vinegar
1½ cups whipping cream
2 pints strawberries, washed, hulled, halved

Preheat oven to 250°. Line baking sheet with foil or parchment paper. Use bowl or round baking dish as template and draw 10-inch wide circle on foil or paper. Set aside.

Beat egg whites in bowl on high speed until soft peaks form. Gradually add 1½ cups sugar and continue to beat until mixture is white and glossy with soft peaks, about 10 minutes. Add vinegar and beat at high speed for additional 5 minutes.

With small, flexible spatula, spread meringue mixture inside circle on baking sheet. Keep sides straight and top as flat as possible. Draw spatula up sides of meringue circle to form "ribs". (This will give a finished look and add strength once meringue is baked.)

Bake for 1 hour. Turn oven off and leave pavlova in oven for additional 2 hours. When ready to assemble, carefully remove meringue base from foil or paper and place on serving plate.

Beat whipping cream with remaining ½ cup sugar in bowl until soft peaks form and spread whipped cream evenly over surface of meringue base. Arrange strawberries attractively on top and serve. Serves 12 to 16.

Best Pavlova with Creamy Topping

10 large egg whites
1 tablespoon white vinegar
2¼ cups sugar
2½ tablespoons cornstarch

Preheat oven to 275°. Beat egg whites in bowl on low speed. (Make sure there is absolutely no yolk in the egg whites.) Add vinegar and a pinch of salt while mixing on low.

In separate bowl, combine sugar and cornstarch; add mixture gradually to egg whites and beat on low until well incorporated. Turn speed to high and beat for 5 minutes or until stiff peaks form.

Spread sprayed parchment paper on baking sheet and spoon egg mixture onto paper. Form mixture into 10-inch circle and flatten top.

Place baking sheet in oven for 10 minutes or until shell forms. Reduce heat to 240° and continue cooking for about 1 hour or until meringue begins to crack. (Do not brown.) Cool meringue completely.

Topping:

1 pint whipping cream
¾ cup sugar
1 teaspoon vanilla
Fresh fruits

Beat whipping cream in bowl and gradually add sugar and vanilla. Beat until stiff peaks form. Spread whipped cream mixture over meringue and place slices of fresh peaches, mango, kiwi, banana or any other fresh fruit you like. (Do not top meringue with whipped cream and fruit until just before serving.) Serves 14.

Flan

2 tablespoons butter
1 cup sugar, divided
1 (14 ounce) can sweetened condensed milk
1 (13 ounce) can evaporated milk
4 eggs, very well beaten
1 teaspoon vanilla

Preheat oven to 350°.

Rub butter in heavy saucepan on bottom and sides. Melt ½ cup sugar in saucepan over medium heat until it carmelizes. Add remaining sugar and stir until there is clear brown syrup. Pour equal parts into 6 individual, custard bowls.

Combine sweetened condensed milk, evaporated milk, eggs and vanilla in bowl and mix well. Pour mixture over cooled, melted sugar mixture in custard bowls. Place bowls in another container half-filled with water.

Bake for 1 hour. Flan is done when toothpick inserted in center comes out clean. Serve by carefully turning bowls upside-down onto plate and removing flan from bowls. The caramelized sugar will be on top. Serves 6.

Flan was a favorite in ancient Rome when domesticated chickens were first kept as egg layers. This form of custard spread through Europe and has become popular in Spain and Mexico.

Ladyfingers

½ cup sifted cake flour
⅔ cup powdered sugar, divided
3 eggs, separated
½ teaspoon vanilla

Preheat oven to 350°. Mix and sift flour, ⅛ teaspoon salt, and ⅓ cup powdered sugar in bowl. Beat egg whites until stiff and gradually beat in remaining powdered sugar.

Fold in vanilla and well beaten egg yolks beaten until thick and very light colored. Carefully fold in flour-powdered sugar mixture, sprinkling about 3 tablespoons at a time.

Press through pastry tube on cookie sheet or silpat, making strips 4 x 1-inch or bake in ladyfinger pans. Dust with additional powdered sugar and bake for 10 to 12 minutes. Batter may be dropped from teaspoon to make rounds if desired. Yields 24 ladyfingers.

TIP: Delicious served with fruit and whipped cream.

Cream Puffs

½ cup butter at room temperature
1 cup boiling water or milk
1 cup flour
4 eggs

Preheat oven to 400°. Add butter to milk in saucepan and bring to a boil. Add flour all at once and stir vigorously until ball forms in center of pan. Cool slightly.

Add eggs, one at a time, beating after adding each egg and 1 teaspoon salt. Mixture should be very stiff. Shape on sprayed baking sheet by dropping from spoon or using pastry bag and tube.

Bake for 15 minutes. Reduce temperature to 325° and continue baking for 30 minutes or until toothpick inserted in center comes out clean. The puffs should be hollow and dry. Cool.

Fill with Cream Filling (page 91), ice cream or whipped cream. Yields 2 dozen small puffs.

Measure liquids in a clear glass or plastic measuring cup at eye level to insure accuracy.

Eclairs

½ cup butter at room temperature
1 cup boiling water or milk
1 cup flour
4 eggs

Preheat oven to 400°. Add butter to milk in saucepan nd bring
to a boil. Add flour all at once and stir vigorously until ball forms
in center of pan. Cool slightly.

Add eggs, one at a time, beating after adding each egg and
1 teaspoon salt. Mixture should be very stiff. Press dough through
pastry bag and tube onto sprayed shallow pan in strips of 4 inches
long and 1-inch wide.

Bake for 15 minutes. Reduce temperature to 325° and continue
baking for 30 minutes or until toothpick inserted in center comes
out clean. The puffs should be hollow and dry. Cool.

Fill with Cream Filling (page 91), ice cream or whipped cream.
Yields 2 dozen small puffs.

*Like many foods, the exact origin of the eclair is uncertain, but
it seems to have been made in France around the beginning of the
19th century.*

Chocolate Eclairs

½ cup butter at room temperature
1 cup boiling water or milk
1 cup flour
4 eggs

Preheat oven to 400°. Add butter to milk in saucepan and bring to a boil. Add flour all at once and stir vigorously until ball forms in center of pan. Cool slightly.

Add eggs, one at a time, beating after adding each egg and 1 teaspoon salt. Mixture should be very stiff. Press dough through pastry bag and tube onto sprayed shallow pan in strips of 4 inches long and 1-inch wide.

Bake for 15 minutes. Reduce temperature to 325° and continue baking for 30 minutes or until toothpick inserted in center comes out clean. The puffs should be hollow and dry. Cool.

Fill with Chocolate Cream Filling (page 92), ice cream or whipped cream. Yields 2 dozen small puffs.

Originally, only the wealthy could afford chocolate on a regular basis, but Milton Hershey founded his company to produce chocolate at reasonable prices.

Individual Meringues

1(1 pound) box powdered sugar
6 egg whites, room temperature
1 teaspoon cream of tartar
½ teaspoon vanilla
1 teaspoon vinegar

Preheat oven to 250°. Beat powdered sugar and egg whites in bowl at high speed for 10 minutes. Add cream of tartar, vanilla and vinegar and beat for additional 10 minutes.

Spoon individual meringues about 5 inches round on sprayed cookie sheet. Bake for 15 minutes. Raise temperature to 300° and bake for additional 12 minutes. Remove immediately from cookie sheet and store between sheets of wax paper in airtight containers. Yields 12 meringues.

Maple-Cinnamon Pecans

1 egg white
½ teaspoon maple flavoring
2 cups pecan halves
⅔ cup sugar
½ teaspoon ground cinnamon

Preheat oven to 225°. Beat egg white, ½ teaspoon cold water and maple flavoring in bowl until frothy, but not stiff. Add pecans and stir gently until pecans are well coated. Add sugar, ¼ teaspoon salt and cinnamon and mix well.

Place on large pan or baking sheet with sides. Bake for 1 hour and stir every 15 minutes. Yields 2 cups.

Baked Apples

6 apples
6 tablespoons brown sugar

Preheat oven to 350°. Select smooth apples of uniform size. Wash and remove cores. Fill center of each with 1 tablespoon brown sugar. Place in baking dish.

Add enough boiling water to cover bottom of dish. Bake, basting frequently with dish liquor until tender for about 20 to 40 minutes, depending on size and variety of apple.

A little lemon juice or cinnamon may be added to water, if desired.

There are several alternates for brown sugar as a filling, such as strips of bananas, marmalade, preserves, honey, lemon juice, hard cinnamon candy, fresh berries, candied orange peel, chopped pineapple, chopped peach, preserved ginger or nuts. Baked apples may be served with whipped cream. Serves 6.

John Chapman, who became known as Johnny Appleseed, planted apple orchards across the Midwest in Ohio, Indiana, Illinois and Michigan in the early 1800's.

Apple Fritters

1 cup flour
1½ teaspoons baking powder
2 tablespoons sugar
½ cup milk
1 egg
5 - 6 tart apples, such as Granny Smith
Canola oil
Powdered sugar

Mix and sift flour, baking powder, sugar and ½ teaspoon salt in bowl. Add milk and well beaten egg. Mix well. Peel and core apples. Cut in sections.

Dip each piece of apple in batter and fry in deep hot oil (340° to 375°) until brown. If you don't have a thermometer for your oil, just heat oil until drop of water splatters if dropped in oil. Drain on paper towels and sprinkle with powdered sugar. Serves 8.

Baked Applesauce

12 tart cooking apples
½ cup sugar
½ teaspoon ground nutmeg

Preheat oven to 350°. Wash, peel, core and divide apples into eighths. Place in sprayed baking dish. Half cover with water. Sprinkle with sugar and nutmeg.

Cover tightly and bake for 2 hours 30 minutes to 3 hours. Remove and scrape through a sieve or mash. Serves 6.

Peach or Apricot Fritters

1 cup flour
1½ teaspoons baking powder
2 tablespoons sugar
½ cup milk
1 egg
6 large peaches or 10 to 12 apricots
Canola oil
Powdered sugar

Mix and sift flour, baking powder, sugar and ½ teaspoon salt in bowl. Add milk and well beaten egg. Mix well. Peel and pit peaches or apricots. Cut in sections.

Dip each piece of peach in batter and fry in deep hot oil (340° to 375°) until brown. If you don't have a thermometer for your oil, just heat oil until drop of water splatters if dropped in oil. Drain on paper towels and sprinkle with powdered sugar. Serves 8.

Baked Fresh Pears

1 quart Sheldon or Seckel pears
½ cup maple sugar
½ cup packed brown sugar
¼ teaspoon ground ginger

Preheat oven to 300°. Wash pears and put in baking dish or earthen pot, whole with peels. Add remaining ingredients and ½ cup hot water.

Cover and bake for 1 hour 30 minutes. Add water as needed to prevent burning and to make syrup at bottom of pot. May be served over ice cream or with whipped cream. Serves 8.

Apple Crisp

3 pounds tart apples, such as Granny Smith
2 tablespoons freshly squeezed lemon juice
½ cup packed brown sugar
½ teaspoon ground cinnamon
½ teaspoon ground nutmeg
⅓ cup flour
⅓ cup old-fashioned oats
4 tablespoons cold butter
½ cup chopped walnuts (optional)

Preheat oven to 375°. Peel, core and chop apples. Toss with lemon juice in bowl and set aside. In separate bowl, combine brown sugar, cinnamon, nutmeg, flour and oats.

Cut butter into small pieces and then work it into sugar-flour mixture with spoon or in stand mixer until mixture looks like crumbs. Add in nuts, if desired. Spray 9 x 9-inch baking dish. Arrange apples and sprinkle butter-flour mixture over top.

Bake for 30 to 45 minutes or until tender. Serve alone or with ice cream. Serves 8.

Toasting brings out the flavors of nuts and seeds. Place nuts or seeds on baking sheet and bake at 225° for 10 minutes. Be careful not to burn them.

Baked Peaches

3 nearly ripe peaches
½ tablespoon lemon juice
2 tablespoons brown sugar

Preheat oven to 350°. Bring medium saucepan filled with water to a boil. Drop peaches in water for 1 minute or so, until skin bursts and starts to come away from fruit. Quickly remove fruit from boiling water and run them under cold water, removing skins completely.

Let peaches cool for a few minutes, then cut in half and remove the pit. Put peaches, flat-side down in baking pan, being careful that they do not touch one another. Sprinkle with lemon juice and brown sugar. Bake until brown, adding a little syrup if they seem too dry. Serves 3.

Baked Ginger Peaches

5 - 6 whole, nearly ripe peaches
½ cup packed brown sugar
2 teaspoons diced fresh ginger
2 tablespoons butter

Preheat oven to 350°. Bring water to a boil in medium saucepan. Add peaches. Let them boil for about 1 minute until their skins burst. Remove peaches, plunge into cold water and peel.

Put peaches cut-side up in shallow baking dish. Sprinkle with brown sugar and ginger. Dot with butter. Add ½ cup water. Bake for 15 to 20 minutes or until brown. Serves 5 to 6.

Baked Peaches on French Toast

2 large peaches
¾ cup sugar
Juice of ½ lemon, about 2 tablespoons
Peel of 1 lemon, chopped
2 tablespoons butter
4 slices bread, ¼ inch thick
1 egg, well beaten
¼ cup milk
1 tablespoon honey

Preheat oven to 350°. Peel, halve and remove stone from peaches. Dissolve sugar in ¾ cup water in saucepan over medium-low heat. Add peaches and simmer gently until tender, but not mushy.

Remove peaches from syrup to sprayed baking dish. To syrup, add lemon juice and lemon peel, and boil for 5 minutes. Pour syrup over peaches. Dot peaches with butter.

Bake for 30 minutes, basting frequently with syrup. Cut bread in halves, diagonally. Mix egg, milk, honey and ⅛ teaspoon salt in bowl. Dip bread in mixture.

Saute bread on both sides in sprayed pan over medium-high heat. Put on hot platter. Put peaches on top of bread. Add pan syrup. Serves 4.

Candies

M aking candy can be broken down into two or three basic steps. The first involves making some sort of sugar syrup. This is usually a combination of sugar or corn syrup and water. This solution is then heated to a very specific temperature. Most candy syrup needs to be cooked to one of following five stages:

Soft Ball	236° to 240°
Firm Ball	242° to 248°
Hard Ball	250° to 265°
Brittle	270° to 290°
Very Brittle	295° to 310°

The names correspond to how the sugar mixture would act when dropped in cold water. A mixture at 240° should form a soft ball in cold water, while a mixture at 295° should be very brittle. It is possible to test candy in this way without the use of a candy thermometer. However, for beginning candy makers, a thermometer is essential. The temperature can change very quickly and it isn't always possible to test the syrup in water again and again.

The next stage involves adding some sort of flavoring, such as cream, nuts, or chocolate. This can happen at several different stages of the cooking.

Because the steps in a candy recipe can happen quickly and require an immediate response, it helps to have all of the tools ready and all of the ingredients measured before beginning.

Making the sugar syrup may take some practice. If the sugar becomes brittle, when the recipe called for a firm ball, don't panic. Just try it again, keeping a close eye on the thermometer.

Chocolate Fudge

2 cups sugar
⅔ cup milk
2 tablespoons corn syrup
3 ounces dark chocolate, broken in small pieces
2 tablespoon butter or fat
1 teaspoon vanilla

Place sugar, milk, syrup and chocolate in saucepan. Stir until sugar is dissolved. Cook slowly until temperature reaches 236° or until mixture forms soft-ball when a little is dropped into cold water. Remove from heat. Add butter.

When cooled to lukewarm, add vanilla. Beat until thick. Pour into sprayed 9-inch square pan. Refrigerate. Cut into squares when firm. Yields 20 squares.

Molasses Fudge

1 cup sugar
1 cup packed brown sugar
½ cup cream
¼ cup molasses
¼ cup melted butter
2 ounces dark chocolate, grated
1½ teaspoons vanilla

Combine sugar, brown sugar, cream, molasses and butter in saucepan. Bring to a boil and boil for 2 minutes. Add chocolate.

Boil for additional 5 minutes longer, stirring until well blended and then only enough to prevent burning. Remove from heat. Add vanilla. Stir until creamy. Turn into sprayed 9-inch square pan. Refrigerate. Yields 20 squares.

Butterscotch

¼ cup molasses
2 cups packed brown sugar
1 tablespoon cider vinegar
½ cup butter at room temperature

Combine molasses, brown sugar and vinegar in saucepan. Bring to boiling point, stirring only until brown sugar is dissolved. Boil for 2 minutes. Add butter.

Cook to 290° or until syrup becomes brittle when dropped in cold water. Turn into sprayed 9-inch square pan. Cool.

Before butterscotch completely hardens, cut into small rectangles. Refrigerate. Serves 6.

Vanilla Caramels

2 cups sugar
1 cup packed brown sugar
1 cup light corn syrup
1 cup condensed milk
1½ cups milk
⅓ cup butter at room temperature
1½ teaspoons vanilla

Cook sugar, brown sugar, corn syrup, condensed milk and milk in saucepan, stirring constantly until sugar is dissolved. Cook slowly over low heat, stirring occasionally to prevent burning, until the temperature is 248° or until mixture forms a firm ball when tested in cold water.

Remove from heat, add butter, ¼ teaspoon salt and vanilla and mix well. Pour into sprayed pan. When cold remove from pan, cut in cubes and wrap each caramel in wax paper. Serves 12.

Chocolate Caramels

2 cups sugar
1 cup packed brown sugar
1 cup light corn syrup
1 cup condensed milk
1½ cups milk
⅓ cup butter at room temperature
5 ounces dark chocolate, melted
1½ teaspoons vanilla

Cook sugar, brown sugar, corn syrup, condensed milk and milk in saucepan, stirring constantly until sugar is dissolved. Cook slowly over low heat, stirring occasionally to prevent burning, until the temperature is 248° or until mixture forms a firm ball when tested in cold water.

Remove from heat, add butter, dark chocolate, ¼ teaspoon salt and vanilla and mix well. Pour into sprayed pan. When cold remove from pan, cut in cubes and wrap each caramel in wax paper. Serves 10.

Nut Brittle

2 cups sugar
¼ teaspoon baking soda
1 teaspoon vanilla
2 cups nuts

Heat sugar gradually in frying pan. Stir constantly with wooden spoon until golden syrup is formed. Remove from heat immediately, before sugar darkens more.

Quickly stir in ¼ teaspoon salt, baking soda and vanilla. Pour syrup over layer of nuts in sprayed pan. When cold, crack into small pieces. Serves 10.

Chocolate Truffles

¾ cup (1½ sticks) butter
¾ cup cocoa
1 (14 ounce) can sweetened condensed milk
3 tablespoons rum
1 cup finely chopped pecans, divided

Melt butter in small saucepan and stir in cocoa until smooth. (Make sure all lumps are gone.) Stir constantly while slowly adding sweetened condensed milk. Continue to stir and cook mixture for about 5 minutes until it thickens and is smooth and shiny. Remove from heat and stir in rum and ¾ cup pecans.

Pour into baking pan and refrigerate for several hours until mixture is firm enough to shape. Remove mixture from pan by tablespoonfuls and shape into 1-inch balls. Roll in remaining chopped pecans, put on plate and refrigerate several more hours before serving. Serves 8.

Chocolate Marshmallows

4 ounces milk chocolate
32 marshmallows
½ cup shredded coconut

Place chocolate in double boiler and heat slowly until chocolate is melted. Quickly dip marshmallows into chocolate, roll at once in coconut and place on buttered plate. Refrigerate. Serves 6.

Black Walnut Molasses Taffy

1½ cups sugar
½ cup molasses
2 tablespoons cider vinegar
½ teaspoon cream of tartar
4 tablespoons butter
¼ teaspoon baking soda
1 cup black walnut pieces

Boil sugar, molasses, 1½ cups water, vinegar and cream of tartar in saucepan to soft-crack stage 270°. Add butter, ⅛ teaspoon salt and baking soda and pour into sprayed pan.

When cool enough to handle, pull until light in color. Add nuts and work them into mass by kneading and pulling.

Pull into strips the desired thickness and cut into pieces about 1 inch long with scissors. If desired, wrap pieces in wax paper. Serves 10.

Lollipops

2 cups sugar
⅛ teaspoon cream of tartar
Any desired flavoring (such as peppermint, strawberry, or grape)
Coloring, if desired
Wooden sticks

Combine sugar and cream of tartar with ⅔ cup water in saucepan. Stir until sugar is dissolved. Boil until temperature of 290° is reached or until drop of mixture will become hard when dropped into cold water. Remove from heat.

Add flavoring and coloring. Pour into sprayed pans or molds. When partly cooled, insert wooden sticks. Refrigerate. Serves 6.

Chocolate-Coconut Kisses

1 tablespoon sifted flour
1½ cups sifted powdered sugar
3 egg whites
1 teaspoon vanilla
1 7-ounce bar semi-sweet chocolate, cut in pieces
½ cup shredded coconut

Preheat oven to 450°. Sift flour and powdered sugar in bowl. Beat egg whites until they stand in peaks. Gradually sprinkle powdered sugar-flour mixture over egg whites, beating constantly.

Add vanilla, chocolate and coconut. Drop teaspoonfuls of mixture onto sprayed baking sheet and bake for 10 minutes. Yields 4 dozen kisses.

Popcorn Balls

1¼ cups sugar
1¼ cups packed brown sugar
½ cup light corn syrup
1 tablespoon butter or fat
14 cups popped corn

Put sugar, brown sugar, syrup and ⅔ cup water in saucepan, stirring until sugar is dissolved. Add butter and continue cooking, without stirring, until temperature reaches 240° or until mixture forms a soft-ball when tested in cold water.

Put popped corn in large bowl and sprinkle with 1¼ teaspoons salt. Pour hot syrup over and mix thoroughly with wooden spoon. When it has cooled slightly, shape into small balls and wrap in wax paper. Yields 14 balls.

Caramel Crunch

½ cup firmly packed brown sugar
½ cup light corn syrup
4 tablespoons butter
6 cups bite-size crispy corn cereal
2 cups peanuts

Preheat oven to 250°. Heat sugar, syrup and butter in large saucepan. Heat until sugar and butter melt, stirring constantly. Add cereal and peanuts and stir until all ingredients are well coated.

Spread mixture on sprayed cookie sheet and bake for 30 minutes. Stir occasionally white baking. Cool and store in airtight container. Serves 6 to 8.

Baked Caramel Corn

1 cup (2 sticks) butter
2 cups packed brown sugar
½ cup light or dark corn syrup
½ teaspoon baking soda
1 tablespoon vanilla
6 quarts popped corn
Peanuts, optional

Preheat oven to 250°. Melt butter in saucepan and stir in brown sugar, corn syrup and 1 tablespoon salt. Stir constantly and bring to a boil. Boil but do not stir for 5 minutes. Remove from heat and stir in baking soda and vanilla. Pour mixture over popped corn and mix well.

Turn into 2 large shallow baking pans and bake for 1 hour. Stir every 15 minutes. Remove from oven and cool completely. Break apart and store in sealed containers. Yields 6 quarts.

Cracker Candy Bites

2¾ cups round buttery crackers
¾ cup (1½ sticks) butter
2 cups packed brown sugar
1 (12 ounce) package milk chocolate chips

Preheat oven to 350°. Place crackers in sprayed 9 x 13-inch baking dish.

Combine butter and brown sugar in saucepan and bring to a boil. Boil for 3 minutes, stir constantly and pour over crackers. Bake for 5 minutes and TURN OVEN OFF.

Sprinkle chocolate chips over cracker mixture. Return to oven and let stand for about 5 minutes or until chocolate melts.

Remove from oven and spread chocolate evenly over cracker mixture. Cool and break into pieces. Yields 1 quart.

Milk chocolate was first made in Switzerland in 1875 and the world of candy hasn't been the same since!

Nutty Haystacks

1 pound candy orange slices, chopped
2 cups flaked coconut
2 cups chopped pecans
1 (14 ounce) can sweetened condensed milk
2 cups powdered sugar

Preheat oven to 350°.

Place orange slices, coconut, pecans and sweetened condensed milk in saucepan and cook for 12 minutes or until bubbly.

Add powdered sugar and mix well. Drop teaspoonfuls of mixture onto wax paper. Serves 10 to 14.

The ancient Egyptians, Greeks, Romans, Chinese, Indians all made preserves and confections. Sugar was used as a preservative for fruit. These were primarily treats for the well-to-do. The availability of sugar for everyone is a relatively recent development in the last two centuries.

Easy, No-Fail Divinity

2½ cups sugar
½ cup light corn syrup
2 egg whites, stiffly beaten
1 teaspoon vanilla
¾ cup chopped nuts

Combine sugar, corn syrup, ½ cup water and ⅛ teaspoon salt in saucepan. Boil mixture for about 4 minutes or until soft-ball stage. (234° on candy thermometer)

Beat egg whites in bowl until fairly stiff and slowly pour half syrup into beaten whites (beat constantly). Continue cooking remaining syrup until it reaches crack-stage (270° on candy thermometer).

While still beating on high, slowly pour in remaining syrup. Reduce speed to low and continue beating for additional 5 minutes or until teaspoon of candy stands up. Quickly stir in vanilla and pecans. Drop on sprayed baking sheet. Serves 8 to 12.

By the Middle Ages, physicians had discovered that sugar made bad-tasting medicines easier to take – a practice that still exists in drugs today.

Yeast Breads
&
Quick Breads

**There's nothing quite like the
aroma of freshly baked bread!**

Yeast Breads & Quick Breads Contents

Yeast Breads

Yeast breads are a wonderful addition to any cook's repertoire. Though more time-consuming than baking a quick bread or buying a baguette, making these breads can be relaxing and enjoyable. With just a little practice and a few pointers, yeast breads can be conquered in no time.

Make sure to use fresh yeast. Old yeast may keep a dough from rising properly. If in doubt, buy a new yeast cake or packet. Yeast is inexpensive and it may prevent some heartache.

When activating the yeast, take care to use a lukewarm liquid (about 120° is ideal). A cooler liquid may not activate the yeast sufficiently and a warmer one may kill it. The liquid should feel just slightly warm to the touch.

Once the dough is made, find a nice, warm spot for it to rise. In a drafty kitchen or sub-zero temperatures, try putting the dough in a gas oven with the pilot light (but not the heat) turned on. A heat register or a warm corner of a room will also do. Don't expose the dough to too much heat, though, or it will rise too quickly.

A stand mixer with a dough hook can be a great help when making these breads. The dough hook takes all of the hard work out of kneading and mixing. Kneading by hand, though, can be a pleasure in itself.

Bread I

1 cup milk
3 tablespoons butter
2 tablespoons sugar
1 yeast cake (0.6 ounces) or 1 packet active dry yeast
6½ cups flour

Add 1 cup water to milk in saucepan. Heat. Add butter, sugar and 2½ teaspoons salt. Remove from heat and allow to cool slightly, until mixture is warm to the touch.

Dissolve yeast in ¼ cup lukewarm water and add to mixture. Stir in 3 to 4 cups flour and beat thoroughly. Cover and set in warm place to rise overnight.

In morning add enough flour to make a firm dough. Knead on floured board or in a stand mixer until smooth and elastic to touch.

Cover and set in warm place to rise until it triples in bulk. Knead again. Shape into loaves and place in 2 sprayed loaf pans.

Cover and let rise again until double in bulk. Bake at 350° for 50 to 60 minutes. Yields 2 loafs.

The Egyptians discovered yeast about 1000 B.C. They also developed a wheat from which white flour could be made. This made the first modern bread possible.

Bread II

1 cup milk
2 tablespoons butter
1½ tablespoons sugar
1 yeast cake (0.6 ounces) or 1 packet active dry yeast
2½ cups flour plus more as needed

Heat milk in saucepan. Add butter, sugar and 1½ teaspoons salt. Remove from heat and allow to cool slightly, until the mixture is warm to the touch.

Dissolve yeast in ¼ cup lukewarm water. Add to mixture. Add flour and beat thoroughly. Cover and set in a warm place to rise until doubled, about 1 hour.

Add enough flour to make a firm dough. Knead on a floured board or in a stand mixer until smooth and elastic to touch.

Cover and set in warm place to rise until it triples in bulk. Knead again. Shape into a loaf and place in 2 sprayed loaf pans. Cover and set in a warm place to rise until double in bulk. Bake at 350° for 50 to 60 minutes. Yields 2 loafs.

Some flours such as rye or whole wheat will create a heavier, denser loaf.

French Bread

2 teaspoons sugar
1 yeast cake (0.6 ounces) or 1 packet active dry yeast
12 cups sifted flour
½ teaspoon cornstarch

Blend sugar, 2 teaspoons salt and yeast with a knife or back of spoon in bowl. Add 4 cups lukewarm water. Place flour in separate bowl.

Hollow out center and add liquid mixture. Mix and knead on floured board or in stand mixer until smooth and elastic. Cover and set in warm place to rise until double in bulk, about 4 hours.

Knead or mix again and cover and set in warm place to rise again until doubled in bulk. Mold into 2 long loaves. Put on baking sheets. Cover and again set in warm place to rise until double in bulk.

Bake at 350° for 1 hour 15 minutes to 1 hour 30 minutes. Fifteen minutes before baking is finished, blend cornstarch in 2 teaspoons cold water and boil for 5 minutes in ⅓ cup boiling water. Brush mixture on bread. Yields 2 loafs.

Test the water in which you plan to dissolve yeast by pouring a bit on your wrist. It should be slightly warm – like a baby's bottle. Or use an instant thermometer to see if the temperature is about 110° to 115°.

Raisin Bread

1 cup milk
3 tablespoons butter
4 tablespoons sugar
1 yeast cake (0.6 ounces) or 1 packet active dry yeast
4½ cups flour
1 cup raisins

Heat milk in saucepan. Add butter, sugar and 1 teaspoon salt. Dissolve yeast in 2 tablespoons lukewarm water. Add to mixture once it has cooled. Add 2 cups flour and beat until smooth. Cover and set in warm place to rise for 1 hour.

Add raisins and remaining flour to make a firm dough. Knead or mix in stand mixer until smooth and elastic to touch. Cover and set in warm place to rise until double in bulk.

Knead or mix again. Form into loaf and put in sprayed loaf pan. Cover and set in warm place to rise until doubled in bulk. Bake at 350° for 50 to 60 minutes. Yields 1 loaf.

Whole Wheat Bread

1 cup milk
2 tablespoons butter
¼ cup sugar
1 yeast cake
2 cups flour
1½ - 2 cups whole wheat flour

Heat milk in saucepan and add butter, sugar and 1 teaspoon salt. Dissolve yeast in 2 tablespoons lukewarm water. When milk mixture has cooled, add yeast. Add white flour and beat until smooth. Cover and set in warm plate to rise for about 1 hour.

Add whole wheat flour and knead or mix in stand mixer until it is elastic to touch and does not stick to unfloured board. Cover and set in warm place to rise until double in bulk.

Knead or mix again until free from air bubbles. Put in sprayed loaf pan. Cover and set in warm place to rise until doubled in bulk. Bake at 350° for 50 to 60 minutes. Yields 1 loaf.

Through most of the history of bread, the white breads were more highly prized and more expensive while darker breads were eaten by the lower classes. Today, the dark breads are more valued for both their taste and nutritional qualities.

Cheese Bread

1 cup milk
2 tablespoons butter
¼ cup sugar
1 yeast cake
2 cups flour
⅔ cup shredded cheddar cheese
1½ - 2 cups whole wheat flour

Heat milk in saucepan and add butter, sugar and 1 teaspoon salt. Dissolve yeast in 2 tablespoons lukewarm water. When milk mixture has cooled, add yeast. Add white flour and cheese and beat until smooth. Cover and set in warm plate to rise for about 1 hour.

Add whole wheat flour and knead or mix in stand mixer until it is elastic to touch and does not stick to unfloured board. Cover and set in warm place to rise until double in bulk.

Knead or mix again until free from air bubbles. Put in sprayed loaf pan. Cover and set in warm place to rise until doubled in bulk. Bake at 350° for 50 to 60 minutes. Yields 1 loaf.

If bread has a yeasty or a sour taste, the place where the dough rose may have been too warm, or the dough was allowed to rise too long.

Nut Bread

1 cup milk
2 tablespoons butter
¼ cup sugar
1 yeast cake
2 cups flour
⅔ cup chopped nuts
1½ - 2 cups whole wheat flour

Heat milk in saucepan and add butter, sugar and 1 teaspoon salt. Dissolve yeast in 2 tablespoons lukewarm water. When milk mixture has cooled, add yeast. Add white flour and nuts and beat until smooth. Cover and set in warm plate to rise for about 1 hour.

Add whole wheat flour and knead or mix in stand mixer until it is elastic to touch and does not stick to unfloured board. Cover and set in warm place to rise until double in bulk.

Knead or mix again until free from air bubbles. Put in sprayed loaf pan. Cover and set in warm place to rise until doubled in bulk. Bake at 350° for 50 to 60 minutes. Yields 1 loaf.

If bread is not removed from the pan and cooled on a rack, it may become soggy on the bottom.

Plain Yeast Rolls

½ cup milk
2 tablespoons butter
2 tablespoons sugar
1 yeast cake (0.6 ounces) or 1 packet active dry yeast
1 egg or 2 egg yolks
3½ cups flour

Heat milk in saucepan and add butter, sugar and 2 teaspoons salt. Soften yeast in ½ cup lukewarm water. Cool milk to lukewarm and add yeast and beaten egg. Add flour to make a soft dough.

Turn out on lightly floured board and knead until smooth and satiny. Place in lightly sprayed bowl and cover. Set in warm place and allow to double in bulk.

Punch down and mold into rolls. Cover and set in warm place to rise until double in bulk. Bake at 400° for 15 to 20 minutes. Yields 20 rolls.

Leavening is what makes baked goods rise. There are a number of leavening agents: yeast, baking powder, baking soda, and the emulsion created when eggs are beaten into creamed butter and sugar. All of these put air into the mixture and add lightness to the texture of the finished product.

Refrigerator Rolls

2 yeast cakes (0.6 ounces each) or 2 packets active dry yeasts
¼ cup sugar
1 cup milk
½ cup butter
3 eggs, beaten
5 cups flour

Crumble yeast in bowl and mix with sugar. Let stand for 20 minutes. Heat milk in saucepan. Add butter and 1 teaspoon salt. Cool to lukewarm. Add yeast-sugar mixture and eggs. Add flour, mixing thoroughly.

Turn out on flour board and knead in stand mixer until satiny. Place in sprayed bowl. Cover and set in warm place to rise until double in bulk, about 2 hours.

Knead or mix again. Form into a smooth ball. Spray surface. Cover and keep in refrigerator, or make immediately. Bake rolls at 375° for 15 to 20 minutes. Yields 24 rolls.

If you have stored yeast for a while, it may no longer be active. You can test or "proof" it by dissolving a teaspoon of sugar in warm water (about 110° to 115°) and then whisking in a package (or cake) of yeast. Use the amount of water called for in the recipe or ¼ cup if more is called for. Let stand for about 5 to 10 minutes. If the yeast has begun to form a creamy foam on top, then it is okay and you can combine the yeast mixture with the rest of the ingredients. If no foam forms, then the yeast is inactive (dead) and cannot be used. You will need to start over with fresh yeast.

Sour Cream Rolls

2 cups thick sour cream
1 yeast cake (0.6 ounces) or 1 packet active dry yeast
¼ teaspoon baking soda
¼ cup sugar
4 cups flour
Melted butter

Bring sour cream to a boil in saucepan, remove from heat and cool to lukewarm. Crumble yeast and stir into ⅓ cup lukewarm sour cream.

Add baking soda, 2 teaspoons salt and sugar to remaining cream and mix well. Combine the 2 mixtures and add flour gradually, stirring constantly until smooth. Brush with melted butter.

Cover and put in warm place and let rise to about 2½ to 3 times the original volume. Knead lightly for about one minute and cut dough in 2 parts.

Roll out one part at a time in rectangular shape about ⅛ inch thick. Brush with butter and cut in lengthwise strips about 2 inches wide.

Place strips on top of each other and cut off pieces about 1½ inch wide. Place pieces in small sprayed muffin cups with cut edges up. Let rise in warm place until double in size.

Bake at 375° for 10 to 15 minutes or until golden brown. Brush with butter if desired. Yields 24 rolls.

Pecan Rolls

½ yeast cake (0.3 ounces) or ½ packet active dry yeast
¼ cup sugar, divided
¾ cup butter at room temperature plus more for muffin cups
1 egg, beaten
1 cup lukewarm milk
4 cups sifted flour
1 cup packed brown sugar, divided
1 cup chopped pecans
4 whole pecans

Soften yeast in 2 tablespoons lukewarm water. Add ½ teaspoon sugar. Cream ¼ cup butter in bowl. Add remaining sugar, egg and lukewarm milk. Add yeast.

In separate bowl, mix and sift ¾ teaspoon salt and flour. Stir into first mixture until dough is firm. Knead 10 to 15 minutes on floured board or in stand mixer until smooth and elastic to touch.

Put dough in sprayed bowl. Cover and set in a warm place to rise until doubled in bulk. Knead again. Roll out in rectangular shape ¼ inch thick.

Spread with remaining softened butter. Dredge with brown sugar. Sprinkle with chopped pecans. Roll like jellyroll.

Cut in 1 inch thick slices. Place 4 whole pecans, 2 teaspoons brown sugar, and ½ teaspoon butter in each muffin cup. Press 1 roll into each hard enough to make nuts stick.

Cover and set in warm place to rise until doubled in bulk. Bake at 350° for about 20 minutes, or until light brown. Turn out, bottom-side up so pecans will be on top. Yields 12 rolls.

Coffee Rolls

1 cup milk
¼ cup butter
¼ cup plus 2 tablespoons sugar
1 yeast cake (0.6 ounces) or 1 packet active dry yeast
4 - 5 cups flour
2 eggs
½ teaspoon ground cinnamon
2 tablespoons raisins

Heat milk in saucepan and add butter, ¼ cup sugar and 1 teaspoon salt. When lukewarm, add yeast, dissolved in 2 tablespoons lukewarm water. Add 1½ cups flour and beat well. Cover and set in warm place to rise.

When double in bulk, add beaten eggs and mix well. Add enough flour to make a firm dough. Knead on slightly floured board or in stand mixer until smooth and elastic to touch. Cover and set in warm place to rise until double in bulk.

Knead again. Break off small pieces of dough, shape into balls and flatten like biscuits. Fit into sprayed loaf pan. Cover and set in warm place to rise until tripled in bulk.

Brush tops with melted butter. Sprinkle with remaining sugar, cinnamon and raisins. Bake at 400° for 25 to 30 minutes. Yields 30 rolls.

If bread dough does not rise, the yeast may be old and inactive, the water was too cold to activate the yeast, the water was so hot that it killed the yeast, the dough was too stiff or the dough was not placed in a warm enough place to rise.

Buttermilk Rolls

1 yeast cake (0.6 ounces) or 1 packet active dry yeast
2 cups buttermilk
¼ cup sugar
¼ teaspoon baking soda
¼ cup melted butter
5 cups flour

Soften yeast in ¼ cup lukewarm water. Heat buttermilk in double boiler. Add sugar, 2 teaspoons salt, baking soda and melted butter. Cool to lukewarm.

Add softened yeast and half the flour, beating well. Add enough flour to make a soft dough. Turn out on lightly floured board and knead or mix in stand mixer until satiny.

Shape into small round biscuits and place in sprayed pan or roll out ½ inch thick and cut with biscuit cutter. Brush each round with melted butter, fold over and place on sprayed baking sheet or in shallow pan. Brush lightly with melted butter.

Cover and let rise until double in bulk about 1 hour 30 minutes. Bake at 400° for 15 to 20 minutes. Yields 6 dozen small rolls.

If bread dough rises too high, the bread may fall when baked.

Whole Wheat Muffins

2 cups scalded milk
1 yeast cake (0.6 ounces) or 1 packet active dry yeast
¼ cup packed brown sugar
¼ cup melted butter
1 egg, well beaten
2½ cups whole wheat flour

Cool milk to lukewarm. Add yeast and dissolve. Add brown sugar, butter and egg. Sift flour with ½ teaspoon salt and add it to mixture.

Beat until smooth. Cover and set in warm place to rise until light. Pour into sprayed muffin cups, two-thirds full.

Cover and set in warm place to rise until cups are full. Bake at 350° for 20 to 25 minutes. Yields 12 muffins.

Bread is done if it makes a hollow sound when lightly tapped. When baking is finished, bread should be removed from the pan immediately and allowed to cool on a wire rack.

Potato Rolls

1 cup mashed potatoes
7 cups flour
¾ cup butter at room temperature
½ cup sugar
2 eggs, well beaten
1 cup scalded milk
1 yeast cake (0.6 ounces) or 1 packet active dry yeast

Mix potatoes, 1 cup flour, butter, sugar and ½ teaspoon salt in bowl. Add eggs and milk, cooled to lukewarm. Dissolve yeast in ½ cup lukewarm water and add to first mixture. Cover and set in a warm place to rise 2 hours.

Add remaining flour. Knead, or mix in a stand mixer with a dough hook, until smooth and elastic to the touch. Cover and set in a warm place to rise again for 1 hour 30 minutes.

Knead. Roll ¼ inch thick. Cut with biscuit cutter. Fold and lay with space between on sprayed baking pan. Set in warm place and let rise for 1 hour 30 minutes. Bake at 325° for 20 minutes. Yields 30 rolls.

If bread crumbles easily, the dough may not have been well mixed, the dough was too stiff, it rose for too long a time, the place where it rose was too warm or the temperature was too low in the oven.

English Teacake

1 yeast cake (0.6 ounces) or 1 packet active dry yeast
½ cup hot milk
¼ cup butter at room temperature
¼ cup plus 2 tablespoons sugar
1 egg or 2 egg yolks
½ cup raisins
1½ cups flour
½ teaspoon ground cinnamon
½ cup chopped nuts

Soften yeast in milk in bwol that has been cooled to lukewarm. Add butter, ¼ cup sugar, eggs, ½ teaspoon salt, raisins and flour. (This makes a rather stiff drop batter.) Beat until smooth. Let rise covered in warm place for 2 hours or until doubled in bulk.

Stir down and fill sprayed, 2 inches deep pan about one-half to three-fourths full. Make topping of cinnamon, nuts and remaining sugar. Combine and sprinkle over dough. Let rise until puffy. Bake at 400° for 25 to 30 minutes. Yields 12 teacakes.

While variation adds interest to dishes such as soups, stews and casseroles, baking recipes often require a precise proportion between ingredients. Substitute at your own risk!

Quick Breads and Biscuits

Quick breads are called "quick" because they are made without yeast and do not need to rise before being baked. Instead, they usually contain some combination of baking powder, baking soda, and eggs. These are all leavening agents, which help the bread to rise in a much shorter period of time.

As with all baking, the temperature of the ingredients and the speed with which they are combined is the key to making an excellent quick bread. The ingredients in most of the bread recipes, for instance, should be as close to room temperature as possible. This is especially true for butter and eggs. They will combine more easily with the remaining ingredients and lend additional volume to the batter. This will result in a lighter crumb and tastier bread.

For biscuits, on the other hand, the butter should be quite cold. Butter does not need to be fully incorporated into the dough; a few pea-sized pieces here and there will actually make for a better biscuit.

The dough should also be made quickly and handled as little as possible. Rolling the dough out with strong, swift strokes and immediately getting the biscuits into a hot oven will produce light, fluffy results.

Whether making bread or biscuits, be careful not to overwork the dough. The more a dough is stirred or mixed after the flour has been added, the tougher the end result will be. Having all of the ingredients measured out and at the right temperature is an excellent way to combat this problem.

Homemade Biscuit Mix

8 cups flour
8 teaspoons baking powder
1½ cups butter, chilled

Sift flour with baking powder and 4 teaspoons salt in bowl. Add butter and cut in with knives or pulse in food processor until mixture has a fine even crumb.

Place in closed container and keep in refrigerator, using as desired. This mixture will keep at least 1 month in the refrigerator. It will yield 5 batches with 2 cups of mixture to each batch.

It may be used for biscuits, dumplings, shortcake, waffles, muffins, quick coffee cake and dozens of other things.

Baking Powder Biscuits

2 cups flour
4 teaspoons baking powder
¼ cup butter, chilled
¾ cup milk

Preheat oven to 375°. Sift flour, baking powder and ½ teaspoon salt in bowl Rub butter in with fingertips. Add milk slowly and mix to soft dough.

Roll out on slightly floured board to ½ inch thickness. Cut with biscuit cutter. Bake for 10 to 15 minutes or until nicely brown. Yields 12 biscuits.

Emergency Biscuits

2 cups flour
4 teaspoons baking powder
¼ cup butter, chilled
1 cup milk

Preheat oven to 375°. Sift flour, baking powder and ½ teaspoon salt in bowl. Rub butter in with fingertips. Add milk slowly and mix to soft dough.

Roll out on slightly floured board to ½ inch thickness. Cut with biscuit cutter. Bake for 10 to 15 minutes or until nicely brown. Yields 12 biscuits.

Cream of Tartar Biscuits

3 cups flour
2 teaspoons cream of tartar
1½ tablespoons butter, chilled
1 teaspoon baking soda
1 cup milk

Preheat oven to 375°. Mix and sift flour, 1 teaspoon salt and cream of tartar in bowl. Work in butter with fingertips.

In separate bowl, mix baking soda and milk and add to flour mixture. Mix thoroughly and knead on floured board until satiny. Roll ¾ inch thick.

Cut with biscuit cutter or small glass. Bake on sprayed pan with space between for 15 minutes or until nicely brown. Yields 12 biscuits.

Sour Milk Biscuits

2 cups flour
1 tablespoon baking powder
2 tablespoons butter, chilled
½ teaspoon baking soda
¾ cup sour milk or buttermilk

Preheat oven to 375°. Sift flour, baking powder and 1 teaspoon salt in bowl. Rub in butter with fingertips. In separate bowl, mix baking soda and sour milk.

Add slowly to first mixture and mix to a soft dough. Roll out on slightly floured board to ½ inch thickness. Cut with biscuit cutter. Bake for 10 to 15 minutes. Yields 12 biscuits.

Sweet Potato Biscuits

1 cup mashed sweet potatoes
1 tablespoon butter at room temperature
1 tablespoon sugar
½ teaspoon baking soda
1 cup buttermilk
2 cups flour

Preheat oven to 400°. Beat sweet potatoes, butter and sugar in bowl until well blended. In separate bowl, dissolve baking soda in buttermilk and add to potato mixture.

Mix and sift flour and 1 teaspoon salt and add to first mixture. Mix well. Roll out to ½ inch thickness on floured board.

Cut with small cookie cutter. Put on sprayed baking sheet. Bake for 15 to 20 minutes or until nicely brown. Yields 24 biscuits.

Oatmeal Biscuits

1½ cups flour
1 tablespoon sugar
4 teaspoons baking powder
1½ cups old-fashioned oats
¼ cup butter, chilled
¾ cup milk

Preheat oven to 325°. Sift flour, sugar, baking powder and 1½ teaspoons salt in bowl. Add oats and mix. Rub butter in with fingertips. Add milk slowly and mix to a soft dough.

Roll out on floured board to ¾ inch thickness. Cut with biscuit cutter. Brush tops with milk and bake for 15 to 20 minutes. Yields 15 biscuits.

Sausage Biscuits

2 cups flour
5 teaspoons baking powder
2 tablespoons butter or shortening, chilled
¾ cup milk
8 pan-fried sausage links, fully cooked

Preheat oven to 350°. Mix and sift flour, baking soda and ¾ teaspoon salt in bowl. Rub in butter with fingertips. Add milk gradually, stirring mixture with knife. Roll out on floured pastry cloth to ¾ inch thickness.

Cut into 3-inch round biscuits. Place sausage in center of each biscuit and roll. Place on sprayed baking sheet and bake for 15 minutes. Yields 8 biscuits.

Fluffy Muffins

1 cup milk
1 egg, beaten
¼ cup melted butter
2 cups flour
1 tablespoon baking powder
3 tablespoons sugar

Preheat oven to 375°. Mix milk, egg and butter in bowl. In separate bowl, sift remaining ingredients with ½ teaspoon salt and mix with first mixture lightly. Do not beat.

Pour batter into sprayed muffins cups, two-thirds full and bake for 20 to 25 minutes. Yields 12 muffins.

Bran Muffins

1 cup sifted flour
3½ teaspoons baking powder
3 tablespoons brown sugar
1 cup bran
1 egg, well beaten
⅔ cup milk
3 tablespoons melted butter
¼ cup raisins

Preheat oven to 375°. Mix and sift dry ingredients and ½ teaspoon salt in bowl. Add bran. In separate bowl, combine egg, milk and butter. Add to flour mixture. Then add raisins, stirring only until mixed.

Spray muffin cups and fill them two-thirds full. Bake for 20 to 30 minutes, according to size of muffin. Yields 12 muffins.

Cornmeal Muffins

½ cup cornmeal
1 cup flour
1 tablespoon baking powder
1 tablespoon sugar
¾ cup milk
1 egg, well beaten
1 tablespoon melted butter

Preheat oven to 400°. Mix and sift dry ingredients and
½ teaspoon salt in bowl. Gradually add milk, egg and butter. Bake
in sprayed muffin cups for about 25 minutes. Yields 8 muffins.

Blueberry Muffins

¼ cup butter at room temperature
⅓ cup sugar
2 eggs, well beaten
2 cups flour, divided
5 teaspoons baking powder
⅔ cup milk
½ cup blueberries

Preheat oven to 400°. Cream butter and sugar in bowl.
Add eggs and mix well. In separate bowl, sift 1½ cups flour, baking
powder and 1 teaspoon salt. Add this mixture to first mixture
alternately with milk.

Sprinkle blueberries with remaining flour and stir in lightly.
Bake in sprayed muffin cups for 25 to 30 minutes. Yields
12 muffins.

Sally Lunn Muffins

¼ cup butter at room temperature
⅓ cup sugar
2 eggs, well beaten
2 cups flour, divided
4 teaspoons baking powder
⅔ cup milk

Preheat oven to 400°. Cream butter and sugar in bowl. Add eggs and mix well. In seprate bowl, sift flour, baking powder and 1 teaspoon salt

Add this mixture to first mixture alternately with milk. Bake in sprayed muffin cups for 25 to 30 minutes. Yields 12 muffins.

Quick Fruit Muffins

2 cups Homemade Biscuit Mix (page 239)
¼ cup sugar
1 egg, well beaten
1 cup milk
½ cup dates, nuts, blueberries, sliced cranberries or chopped fruits

Preheat oven to 400°. Combine biscuit mix and sugar in bowl. In seprate bowl, beat egg and milk with fork. Add to dough, combining thoroughly without beating.

Add dates, nuts, etc., singly or in combination, as desired. Pour into sprayed muffin cups. Bake for 20 minutes. Yields 8 muffins.

Banana-Bran Muffins

1 cup flour
½ teaspoon baking soda
1 teaspoon baking powder
2 tablespoons butter at room temperature
¼ cup sugar
1 egg, well beaten
1 cup shredded bran
2 tablespoons milk
2 cups bananas, thinly sliced

Preheat oven to 375°. Sift flour with ½ teaspoon salt, baking soda and baking powder in bowl. In separate bowl, cream butter. Add sugar and cream gradually. Add egg, bran and milk. Mix and allow to stand while slicing bananas.

Add bananas and mix well. Add sifted dry ingredients, stirring as little as possible. Bake in sprayed muffin cups for 20 to 30 minutes. Yields 12 muffins.

Mix muffin batter only until the dry ingredients are moist and the batter is still lumpy. If it is mixed until smooth, the muffins will have a tough, heavy texture.

Coconut Bread

This recipe makes a pretty plate of red and white sandwiches.

1¼ cups shredded coconut
2⅔ cups flour
1¼ cups sugar
4 teaspoons baking powder
1½ cups milk
1 egg
2 tablespoons canola oil
1¼ teaspoons coconut extract

Preheat oven to 300°. Place coconut on baking sheet and bake for 15 minutes. Shake pan and stir 2 times so that it will toast evenly. Remove from oven and cool.

Increase oven heat to 350° and spray 9 x 5-inch loaf pan.

Sift flour, sugar, baking powder and 1 teaspoon salt in bowl and stir in coconut. In separate bowl, combine milk, egg, oil and coconut extract. Beat to blend egg into milk. Add liquid mixture to dry ingredients all at once and mix well, but do not over mix.

Pour batter into loaf pan and bake for 1 hour 5 minutes. Bread is done when toothpick inserted in center comes out clean. Cool. To serve, cut in thin slices and spread with Strawberry Butter. Place another slice on top. Cut in 3 strips.

Strawberry Butter

1¼ cups powdered sugar
1 (10 ounce) package frozen strawberries, thawed, drained
1 cup (2 sticks) butter, softened

Place all ingredients in food processor and process until well blended. Refrigerate and spread on bread. Serves 8.

Apple Gems

¼ cup butter at room temperature
2 tablespoons sugar
⅔ cup yellow cornmeal
1¼ cups warm milk
1 egg, well beaten
1 cup flour
2 teaspoons baking powder
1½ cups chopped apples

Preheat oven to 350°. Add butter, sugar and cornmeal to milk in bowl and mix well. Add egg, blending well. In separate bowl, sift flour, baking powder and 1 teaspoon salt.

Fold in gently to cornmeal mixture, stirring as little as possible to combine. Add apples to batter and stir thoroughly. Drop into sprayed muffin cups and bake for 25 to 30 minutes. Yields 12 to 14 muffins.

Wheat Sticks

1 cup flour
½ cup whole wheat flour
½ teaspoon baking soda
1 tablespoon sugar
1½ tablespoons butter, chilled

Preheat oven to 350°. Mix and sift flours, 1 teaspoon salt, baking soda and sugar in bowl. Work butter in with fingertips or pulse in food processor until as fine as coarse cornmeal. Add ⅓ cup water gradually, stirring constantly.

Mix well and knead for a few moments on floured board. Roll to ½ inch thickness. Cut into 3 inches by ¼ inch strips. Place on sprayed baking sheet with space between and bake until golden brown, turning once. Yields 12 sticks.

Cheese Straws

Basic Pastry (page 11)
Cayenne
1 cup shredded cheese

Preheat oven to 400°. Roll out pastry to ⅛ inch thickness. Sprinkle with a little salt, cayenne and cheese. Fold in 3 layers. Roll out again.

Cut in strips ½ inch wide and 4 or 5 inches long. Bake for 5 or 6 minutes. Serves 8.

Cheese Fingers

1 cup flour
½ teaspoon baking powder
⅛ teaspoon cayenne pepper
2 tablespoons butter
4 tablespoons shredded cheese

Mix and sift flour, baking powder, cayenne pepper and ½ teaspoon salt in bowl. Cut in butter with knife or pulse in food processor. Add cheese and enough cold water to hold mixture together. Refrigerate for at least 1 hour.

When ready to bake, preheat oven to 400°. Roll out on floured board to ¼ inch thickness. Cut in very thin strips with a knife. Bake for 20 minutes. Yields 50 fingers.

Corn Sticks

1 cup sifted flour
1 cup cornmeal
½ teaspoon baking soda
1 egg, beaten
1 cup sour milk or buttermilk
1 tablespoon melted butter

Preheat oven to 375°. Mix and sift flour, cornmeal, baking soda and 1 teaspoon salt in bowl. In separate bowl, combine egg and milk. Add to flour mixture, stirring until well mixed. Stir in butter. Cut into 3 inches by ¼ inch strips.

Bake on sprayed baking sheet for 15 to 20 minutes. To use regular milk instead of sour milk, substitute 1 tablespoon baking powder for baking soda. For cornbread, bake in sprayed, shallow pan at 400° for about 30 minutes. Yields 12 corn sticks.

Cornbread

1½ cups milk
1 cup cornmeal
1½ tablespoons butter
2 eggs, beaten
1½ teaspoons baking powder
2 teaspoons sugar

Preheat oven to 400°. Heat milk in saucepan and pour over cornmeal and butter. Cool. Add eggs, baking powder, ½ teaspoon salt and sugar. Mix well.

Pour into sprayed 8-inch baking pan and bake for 25 to 30 minutes or until a knife inserted in center comes out clean. Serves 6 to 8.

Date-Nut Bread

1 egg
¼ cup sugar
½ cup crushed walnuts or pecans
½ cup dates, pitted and chopped
2 cups flour
4 teaspoons baking powder
1 cup milk

Preheat oven to 350°. Beat egg and add sugar in bowl. Add nuts and dates. In separate bowl, sift dry ingredients with ½ teaspoon salt and add alternately with milk to first mixture.

Turn into sprayed 9-inch baking pan. Bake for 45 minutes or until knife inserted in center comes out clean. Either all dates or all nuts may be used. Serves 16.

Spoon Bread

1 cup cornmeal
1 tablespoon sugar
1 egg, beaten
½ teaspoon baking soda
1 cup buttermilk or sour milk
1½ tablespoons butter

Preheat oven to 375°. Put cornmeal into bowl. Pour ¾ cup boiling water over cornmeal. Cover and let cool. Add 1 teaspoon salt, sugar and egg.

Dissolve baking soda in buttermilk and add to first mixture. Mix thoroughly. Add butter.

Pour into sprayed 9 x 13-inch baking dish. Bake for 30 to 35. Serves 6 to 8.

Quick Cinnamon Rolls

Baking Powder Biscuits dough (page 239)
2 tablespoons sugar
½ teaspoon ground cinnamon
¼ cup chopped walnuts or pecans

Preheat oven to 375°. Roll biscuit dough ½ inch thick. Spread with mixture of sugar and cinnamon. Roll like jellyroll.

Cut slices ¾ inch thick. Bake for 10 to 15 minutes. Yields 12 rolls.

TIP: *Chopped nuts may be added to the sugar-cinnamon mixture.*

Dumplings

2 cups flour
4 teaspoons baking powder
3 tablespoons butter, chilled
¾ cup milk

Sift flour, 1 teaspoon salt and baking powder in bowl. Rub in butter with fingertips or pulse in food processor until as fine as coarse cornmeal. Add milk to make a soft dough.

Drop 1 tablespoon at a time, on chicken or meat stew during last 15 to 20 minutes of cooking. The stockpot must be covered tightly. Do not remove the cover during cooking. Serves 6.

Johnnycake

1 cup cornmeal
2 tablespoons whole wheat flour
1 tablespoon sugar
1½ tablespoons melted butter
1 cup boiling milk
1 egg

Preheat oven to 400°. Sift cornmeal, wheat flour, ½ teaspoon salt and sugar in bowl. Add butter and pour milk in quickly.

Separate egg. Beat white stiff. Beat yolk and fold into white. Add cornmeal mixture and stir in with gentle folding motion.

Drop spoonfuls of batter in rectangular shape onto sprayed baking sheet, leaving ½ inch between each biscuit. Bake for 30 minutes. Yields 12 Johnnycakes.

Bread has often been called the "staff of life" and has been a nutritious food from prehistoric times. Baking is one of the oldest crafts in the world.

Coffee Ring

3 cups flour
⅓ cup plus 1 tablespoon sugar
2 tablespoons baking powder
1 teaspoon salt
¼ cup chilled butter plus 1 tablespoon melted butter
1 egg, beaten
¾ cup milk
¾ cup raisins
½ cup nuts, chopped
Powdered Sugar Frosting (page 94)

Preheat oven to 350°. Mix and sift flour, ⅓ cup sugar, baking powder and 1 teaspoon salt in bowl. Cut in ¼ cup butter with knife or pulse in food processor until mixture is as fine as coarse cornmeal.

Add egg and milk to make a soft dough. Roll out rectangular-shaped piece about ¼ inch thick. Spread lightly with melted butter, sprinkle with raisins, nuts and remaining sugar.

Roll lengthwise like a jellyroll. Bring ends together to make circle and press together.

Put on large sprayed pan and cut gashes around outside edges with scissors, 2 inches apart. Bake for 25 to 30 minutes. Spread top with powdered sugar frosting. Serves 8.

Cream Scones

2 cups flour
½ teaspoon baking soda
2 tablespoons sugar
¼ cup butter, chilled
Grated peel of 1 lemon
¾ cup light cream
4 teaspoons vinegar
1 egg, slightly beaten

Preheat oven to 375°. Sift flour with baking soda, ¾ teaspoon salt and sugar in bowl. Cut in butter, or pulse in food processor until as fine as coarse cornmeal. Add lemon peel.

In separate bowl, combine cream and vinegar. Add to flour mixture stirring quickly to form stiff dough. Knead slightly on slightly floured board. Roll out ⅜ inch thick.

Cut in diamond shapes. Brush with egg. Place on baking sheet. Bake for 10 to 20 minutes or until nicely brown. Yields 12 scones.

Popovers

1 cup flour
1 cup milk
2 eggs, beaten
1 tablespoon melted butter

Preheat oven to 400°. Spray popover or muffin pan and put it in oven to heat. Mix and sift flour and ¼ teaspoon salt in bowl. Add milk gradually. Add eggs and butter. Beat batter for 5 minutes.

Remove hot pan from oven and pour batter into it. Bake for 30 minutes. Reduce heat to 325° and bake for additional 15 minutes. Do not open oven door for first 15 minutes of baking. Yields 8 to 10 popovers.

Waffles

2 cups flour
4 teaspoons baking powder
1 tablespoon sugar
1¼ cups milk
2 eggs
2 tablespoons melted butter

Sift flour, baking powder, 1 teaspoon salt and sugar in bowl. Add milk. Separate eggs. Beat yolks and add to mixture. Mix thoroughly.

Beat egg whites stiff and fold into mixture. Add butter. Heat waffle iron. Spray well. Put a little batter in center. Close iron.

Waffles are done when they are golden brown all over. Serve with honey, maple syrup or marmalade. Serves 6.

Creamy Pecan Waffles

2 cups flour
1 teaspoon baking soda
1 tablespoon sugar
2 cups sour cream
2 eggs
2 tablespoons melted butter
½ cup chopped pecans

Sift flour, baking soda, 1 teaspoon salt and sugar in bowl. Add sour cream. Separate eggs. Beat yolks and add to mixture. Mix thoroughly.

Beat egg whites stiff and fold into mixture. Add butter and pecans. Heat waffle iron. Spray well. Put a little batter in center. Close iron. Waffles are done when they are golden brown all over. Serve with honey, maple syrup or marmalade. Serves 6.

Date Waffles

2 cups flour
4 teaspoons baking powder
1 tablespoon sugar
1¼ cups milk
2 eggs
2 tablespoons melted butter
1 cup finely chopped nuts

Sift flour, baking powder, 1 teaspoon salt and sugar in bowl.
Add milk. Separate eggs. Beat yolks and add to mixture.
Mix thoroughly.

Beat egg whites stiff and fold into mixture. Add butter and
dates. Heat waffle iron. Spray well. Put a little batter in center.
Close iron. Waffles are done when they are golden brown all over.
Serve with honey, maple syrup or marmalade. Serves 6.

Nutty Waffles

2 cups flour
4 teaspoons baking powder
1 tablespoon sugar
1¼ cups milk
2 eggs
2 tablespoons melted butter
Chopped nuts

Sift flour, baking powder, 1 teaspoon salt and sugar in bowl.
Add milk. Separate eggs. Beat yolks and add to mixture.
Mix thoroughly.

Beat egg whites stiff and fold into mixture. Add butter. Heat
waffle iron. Spray well. Put a little batter in center. Close iron.
Waffles are done when they are golden brown all over. Sprinkle nuts
over each waffle and serve with honey, maple syrup or marmalade.
Serves 6.

Sweet Milk Pancakes

2 cups flour
1½ teaspoons baking powder
2 tablespoons sugar
2 cups milk
1 egg, beaten
1 tablespoon melted butter

Mix and sift flour, 1 teaspoon salt, baking powder and sugar in bowl. Add milk, egg and butter. Mix well.

Drop tablespoonfuls of batter onto hot griddle, sprayed well. Brown on both sides. Serve hot with marmalade or honey. Serves 6.

Banana Pancakes

1½ cups flour
1½ teaspoons baking powder
2 tablespoons sugar
1 cup milk
1 egg, beaten
1 tablespoon melted butter
2 bananas, mashed

Mix and sift flour, 1 teaspoon salt, baking powder and sugar in bowl. Add milk, egg and butter. Mix well.

Stir in bananas and drop tablespoonfuls of batter onto hot griddle, sprayed well. Brown on both sides. Serve hot with marmalade or honey. Serves 6.

Blueberry Pancakes

1 egg
1 cup milk
2 teaspoons baking powder
1 cup flour
½ cup blueberries

Beat egg in bowl until light. Add ¼ teaspoon salt and milk. In separate bowl, sift baking powder with flour and stir it into first mixture. Beat until smooth.

Add blueberries. Drop spoonfuls of batter onto hot griddle and brown both sides. Serves 4.

Jelly Pancakes

1 cup sifted flour
1 teaspoon baking powder
1 teaspoon sugar
2 eggs, separated
1 cup milk
2 tablespoons butter
Jelly

Sift flour, baking powder, ½ teaspoon salt and sugar in bowl. In separate bowl, beat egg yolks and milk with fork. Add gradually to flour mixture, beating only until smooth. Add butter.

Stiffly beat egg whites and gently fold them into batter. Cook on hot, greased griddle. Spread with jelly and roll or roll and serve around fried sausages or bacon. Yields 6 (7-inch) pancakes.

French Toast

2 tablespoons sugar
1 cup whole milk
1 egg, slightly beaten
5 slices of bread

Add ½ teaspoon salt, sugar and milk to slightly beaten egg in bowl. Dip pieces of bread into egg mixture. Cook soaked slices of bread on well sprayed griddle. Brown on one side. Turn and brown on the other. Serve with maple syrup, butter, jam or fruit. Serves 3 to 4.

Cinnamon Toast

Bread
Butter
Sugar
Cinnamon

Spread bread with butter and mixture of 3 parts sugar and 1 part cinnamon. Place on baking sheet and bake at 350° until sugar melts.

Golden Toast Sticks

1 loaf bread
Butter

Preheat oven to 300°. Butter one side of bread and stack each slice on top of each other. Cut stack of about 6 slices into pieces ½ inch wide. Arrange sticks on baking sheet and bake for 20 minutes or until they are crisp throughout and evenly brown. Turn sticks once during baking. Serve with soup, allowing 3 sticks for each person. Serves 8.

Glossary
&
Index

Glossary

Baking

This is cooking in an oven. For best results the temperature of the oven should be regulated exactly as specified in all recipes for baked food.

Beating

Beating can be done manually or with any of several hand operated or electrical devices. Its purpose is to trap air within the food. In general, the motion of food undergoing a beating should be from underneath to the top. Beating should always be vigorously done so that the entire contents are kept constantly in motion.

Blanching

This is plunging into boiling water to either remove a skin or to whiten.

Boiling

This consists of heating water or other liquid until it bubbles rapidly. These bubbles rise to the surface of the liquid and leave it in the form of steam. A liquid, if the steam is permitted to escape freely, can never be heated to a higher temperature than its boiling point. At sea level water boils at 212° F. The temperatures at which water will boil at higher altitudes are shown in the following table:

Altitude in feet	Temperature of boiling water ° F.
1,025	210.99
2,063	208.98
3,115	206.97
4,169	204.95
5,225	202.94
6,304	200.93
7,381	198.92
8,481	196.91
9,031	195.90

The recipes in this book are all based on sea-level conditions. To boil food at 5,000 feet will require a slightly longer time than is stipulated in this book.

Creaming

This is the softening of fat by means of pressure and beating at room temperature. Sugar or other ingredients are often added to the fat during the process of creaming.

Cutting In

This is a method for combining flour and shortening. They are combined in small, crumbly particles by blending them with the fingertips, two knives, or a pastry mixer.

Deep-Fat Frying

This consists of cooking food by immersing it in deep, hot fat or oil. Food cooked by this method should always be placed on a paper towel as soon as it is taken from the fat so that as much fat as possible may be absorbed. If possible, the exact temperature of the fat should be determined by a thermometer.

Dredging

This is the sprinkling of flour or some other dry, pulverized or granulated ingredient. It is often used before frying or roasting a meat or vegetable.

Folding In

This is the process of mixing foods without releasing the air bubbles, which may have been beaten or cooked into any of the ingredients. Folding in is done by lifting a part of the liquid from the very bottom of the bowl through the rest of the mixture to the top. This is continued until the foods are thoroughly blended. This method is commonly used with egg whites.

Kneading

This is the stretching and contraction of dough with the hands as more flour is worked into the mixture. Sometimes kneading is done only to smooth the texture of the dough. It can be done by hand or in a stand mixer.

Measurements

All measurements in this book are level. Follow them exactly. This is a table of equivalent measures:

$$3 \text{ teaspoons} = 1 \text{ tablespoon}$$

$$16 \text{ tablespoons} = 1 \text{ cup}$$

$$2 \text{ cups} = 1 \text{ pint}$$

$$2 \text{ pints} = 1 \text{ quart}$$

$$4 \text{ quarts} = 1 \text{ gallon}$$

Oven Broiling

This consists of cooking foods in the oven of a gas or electric range. The food is placed in the broiler pan and cooked close to the heat.

Pan Broiling

This method calls for the cooking of food on a hot pan or griddle with only enough fat to prevent burning. Any excess fat that accumulates should be poured off at once or the food will fry instead of broil.

Pan Frying

This is frying in a hot pan in a small amount of fat. It differs from pan broiling in that the fat is allowed to accumulate. It differs from sauteing in that the food is not stirred frequently but is simply turned to cook both sides or, as in the case of fried eggs, the food may be cooked on one side only.

Poaching

To poach, foods are dropped into simmering water or other liquid and cooked for a short time. Poaching is used most commonly only for eggs and fish.

Pressure Cooking

To cook by pressure it is necessary to have a pressure cooker manufactured for this purpose. The food is cooked in trapped steam at pressures ranging up to 30 pounds per square inch with temperatures running up to 275°. For most pressure cooking the pressure is kept from 10 to 15 pounds and temperature at 240° to 250°.

Sauteing

This is frying using a little fat in a hot pan. The food is stirred frequently so that the hot grease reaches all sides.

Scalding

This is to heat a liquid briefly to a point just below boiling or to briefly heat a solid food in liquid at the scalding point.

Shortening

This important ingredient in all kinds of batters, pastries and doughs is synonymous with fat. It includes butter, all of the trademarked vegetable fats, margarine, lard, oil or drippings. In most recipes a specific type of shortening is suggested, but it is a matter of personal preference.

Silicone Mat (Silpat)

This is a mat, usually about the size of a cookie sheet, which is made of silicone. It can go in the oven directly on top of a cookie or baking sheet. It is heat resistant and helps foods baked on it to cook more evenly. Foods baked on it can be easily removed as well. It is primarily used for cookies and candies, though it could be used for other things as well.

Simmering

This is heating water or other liquid to a temperature above 175°, but under the boiling point. Bubbles rise infrequently to the surface during simmering.

Stand Mixer

A type of electric mixer in which the bowl is attached to a stand. The beater or hook is attached to the stand as well. It operates with a switch and does not need to be attended to or held while mixing or beating. It can mix, beat, and knead doughs, batters, and other mixtures.

Steaming

Food is steamed when it is cooked in a bath of steam from boiling water. Often a steamer, made of bamboo or metal, sits in the water and holds the food so that it steams rather than boils.

Stewing

Stewing consists of either simmering or boiling food in a small amount of water or liquid.

Stirring

Always stir with a circular motion. It is done either to make certain that heat reaches every part of the food or to thoroughly mix or dissolve ingredients.

Whipping

Whipping is the same as beating, but not as much of it. Its purpose is to put air in a mixture and to increase its volume.

Index

Cookies

D

Puddings

U

Ultimate Fudgy Brownies   169

V

Vanilla Caramels   210

W

Waffles

Waffles   256
Washington Pie   38
Wheat Sticks   248
White Cake   61
Whole Wheat Bread   226
Whole Wheat Muffins   235

Y

Yeast Breads

Yeast Breads   221
Yellow Cake   60
Yummy Cookies   138

Z

Zesty Lemon Squares   161

The warm feelings you create
when you cook with love
will always be treasured
and never forgotten by
your family and friends.

Bringing Family and Friends to the Table

Cookbooks Published
by Cookbook Resources, LLC

Easy Diabetic Recipes

*The Best of Cooking
with 3 Ingredients*

*The Ultimate Cooking
with 4 Ingredients*

Easy Cooking with 5 Ingredients

*Gourmet Cooking
with 5 Ingredients*

*4-Ingredient Recipes
for 30-Minute Meals*

Essential 3-4-5 Ingredient Recipes

The Best 1001 Short, Easy Recipes

1001 Fast Easy Recipes

1001 Community Recipes

*Busy Woman's
Quick & Easy Recipes*

*Busy Woman's
Slow Cooker Recipes*

Easy Slow Cooker Cookbook

Easy One-Dish Meals

Easy Potluck Recipes

Easy Casseroles

Easy Desserts

Sunday Night Suppers

Easy Church Suppers

365 Easy Meals

365 Easy Soups and Stews

365 Easy Vegetarian Recipes

365 Easy Chicken Recipes

365 Easy Soup Recipes

365 Easy One-Dish Recipes

365 Easy Pasta Recipes

365 Easy Slow Cooker Recipes

Quick Fixes with Cake Mixes

*Kitchen Keepsakes/
More Kitchen Keepsakes*

Gifts for the Cookie Jar

All New Gifts for the Cookie Jar

Muffins In A Jar

The Big Bake Sale Cookbook

*Classic Tex-Mex
and Texas Cooking*

Classic Southwest Cooking

Miss Sadie's Southern Cooking

Texas Longhorn Cookbook

Cookbook 25 Years

A Little Taste of Texas

A Little Taste of Texas II

*Trophy Hunters'
Wild Game Cookbook*

Recipe Keeper

*Leaving Home Cookbook
and Survival Guide*

*Classic Pennsylvania
Dutch Cooking*

*Healthy Cooking
with 4 Ingredients*

cookbook resources LLC

www.cookbookresources.com

Your Ultimate Source for Easy Cookbooks

How to Order: **Simple Old-Fashioned Baking**

Order online at www.cookbookresources.com

Or Call Toll Free: (866) 229-2665   Or Mail to: Cookbook Resources
       Fax: (972) 317-6404   541 Doubletree Drive
                                       Highland Village, Texas 75077

> **Please note: Shipping/handling charges may vary according to shipping zone and method.**

Please send ___ copies @ $16.95 (U.S.) each $ _____

Texas residents add sales tax @ $1.40 each $ _____

Plus shipping/handling @ $8.00 (1st copy) $ _____

Plus shipping/handling @ $1.00 per each additional copy $ _____

Check or Credit Card (Canada – credit card only) Total $ _____

Charge to: ☐ MasterCard   ☐ VISA   Expiration Date ⌞__⌟ ⌞__⌟ (mm/yy)

Account No. ⌞__⌟ ⌞__⌟ ⌞__⌟ ⌞__⌟

Signature _____

Name (please print) _____

Address _____

City _____ State/Prov. _____ Zip/Postal Code _____

Telephone (Day) _____ (Evening) _____

How to Order: **Simple Old-Fashioned Baking**

Order online at www.cookbookresources.com

Or Call Toll Free: (866) 229-2665   Or Mail to: Cookbook Resources
       Fax: (972) 317-6404   541 Doubletree Drive
                                       Highland Village, Texas 75077

> **Please note: Shipping/handling charges may vary according to shipping zone and method.**

Please send ___ copies @ $16.95 (U.S.) each $ _____

Texas residents add sales tax @ $1.40 each $ _____

Plus shipping/handling @ $8.00 (1st copy) $ _____

Plus shipping/handling @ $1.00 per each additional copy $ _____

Check or Credit Card (Canada – credit card only) Total $ _____

Charge to: ☐ MasterCard   ☐ VISA   Expiration Date ⌞__⌟ ⌞__⌟ (mm/yy)

Account No. ⌞__⌟ ⌞__⌟ ⌞__⌟ ⌞__⌟

Signature _____

Name (please print) _____

Address _____

City _____ State/Prov. _____ Zip/Postal Code _____

Telephone (Day) _____ (Evening) _____